IOWA FOLK ARTISTS

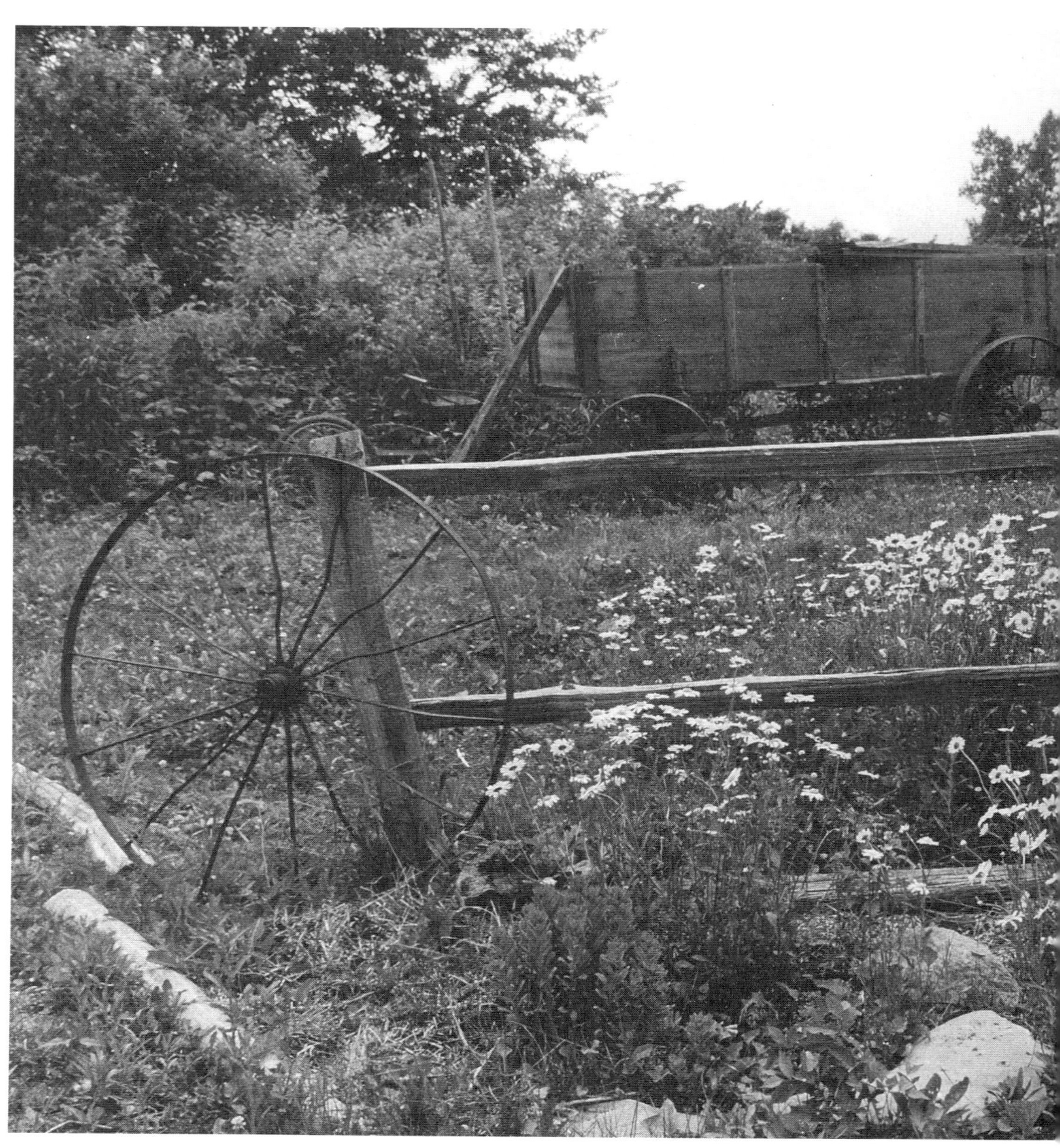

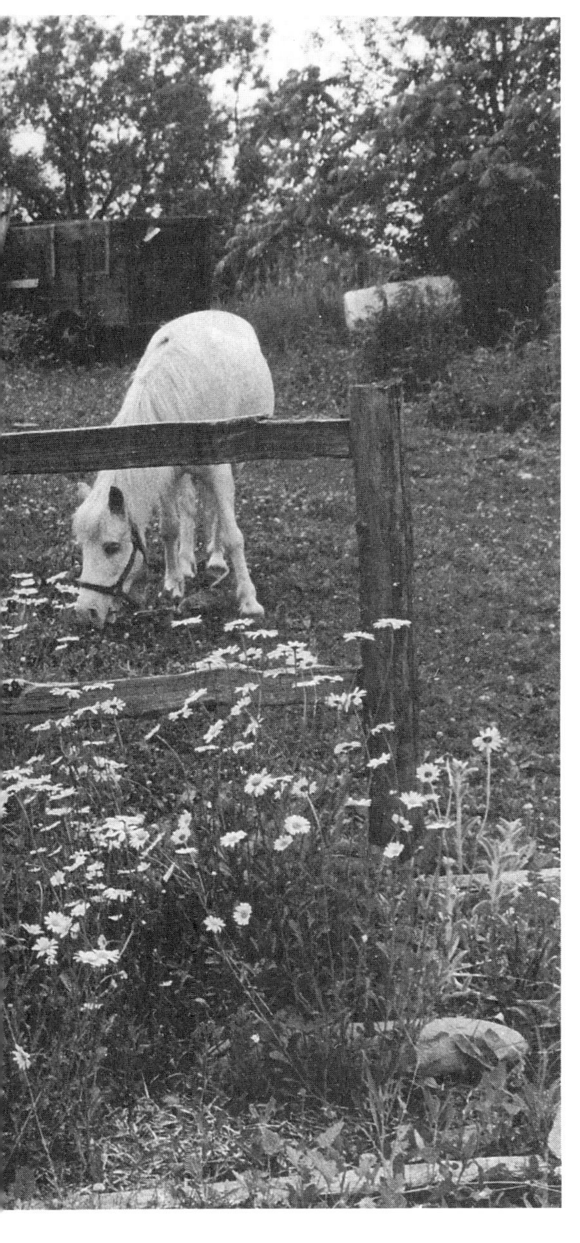

IOWA FOLK ARTISTS

Jacqueline Andre Schmeal

Photographs by Charles Brill

IOWA STATE UNIVERSITY PRESS / AMES

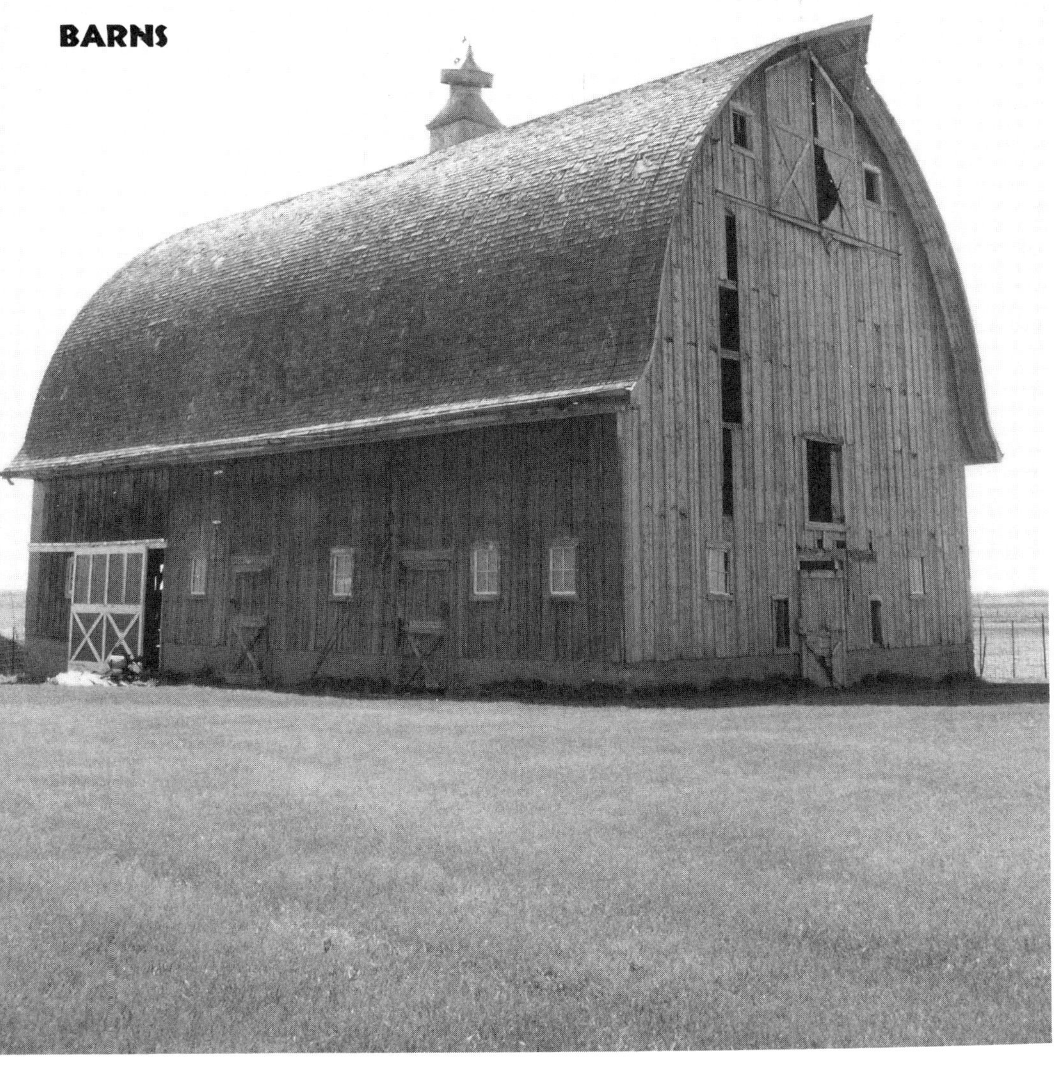

©1998 Iowa State University Press, Ames, Iowa
Photographs © by Charles Brill
All rights reserved

Barn photo, courtesy of Kay Huston

Designed by Kathy J. Walker

Iowa State University Press
2121 South State Avenue, Ames, Iowa 50014

Orders: 1-800-862-6657
Office: 1-515-292-0140
Fax: 1-515-292-3348
Web site: www.isupress.edu

First edition, 1998

Library of Congress Cataloging-in-Publication Data

Schmeal, Jacqueline Andre
Iowa folk artists / Jacqueline Andre Schmeal;
photographs by Charles Brill. — 1st ed.
p.   cm.
Includes bibliographical references.
ISBN 0-8138-2889-9
1. Folk art—Iowa. 2. Folk artists—Iowa—Biography.
I. Brill, Charles.
NK835.I8S36 1998
745' .09777—dc21   98-7575

The last digit is the print number: 9 8 7 6 5 4 3 2 1

CONTENTS

PREFACE

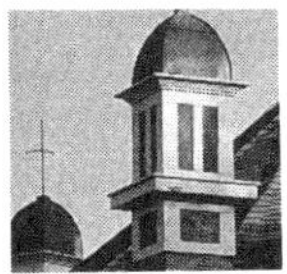 From the time of the first settlers in the 1830s and 1840s, Iowa has been a heart of folk art tied not only to traditions that immigrants from Holland, Sweden, Germany, Norway, and Czechoslovakia carried with them but also to Midwest agriculture and rural life. For relaxation after a day of chores, canning, carrying water, and cooking, women picked up their baskets of handiwork or joined neighbors at a quilt frame. Farmers settling the new land proudly built barns, corncribs, and granaries in styles they knew or created. Beyond the barns, they planted crops artfully and in harmony with the land, creating a unique heritage of agricultural practices and landscape.

As a child growing up in Iowa, I remember sorting through the boxes of crocheted, embroidered, and cross-stitched tablecloths, towels, and napkins that my grandmother had lovingly made through the years. At the foot of my bed was a grandmother's fan quilt that my grandmother had stitched together out of brown calico. Today, I never pass her brown wool and velvet log cabin quilt that adorns our sofa without remembering her and her devotion to fine handiwork, a folk art. My grandmother's hands were never idle until glaucoma took her sight prematurely.

The big white prairie barn on my great-uncle's farm was a center of life. I watched while my great-uncle milked cows and forked hay to the cows and pigs. My great-grandfather had built the barn on a hill overlooking New Sharon in the nineteenth century. It, too, was folk art—something he, an untrained artist, built from his heart. In southern Iowa one farmer wrote proudly on his barn "built by Ole Olson in 1917." A brick silo near Earlham reads: "The 201 Farm, J.H. Williamson, 1919." On top of the silo is a sculptured ear of corn.

All of this—the handiwork, the barns, the way the land was planted—was folk art. It still is. If one uses my definition of *folk art*—art from the heart—then Iowa is a unique center of folk art in America.

It is here where folk artists lead contemporary lives while continuing some of the best traditions from earlier days. They have always worked hard, and they expect to work hard to sustain their crafts. How they lead their lives is looked upon with high regard. Material possessions are not valued as much as the work ethic that is indigenous to Iowa's rural culture.

These down-to-earth folk artists are sincere in their dedication to excellence in their work—and to perpetuating their art. Some, like carvers Harley Refsal and Bill Warrick and rosemaler Ruth Green, are working in an ethnic tradition. Bill Metz and Joanna Schanz are carrying on arts that were important in day-to-day living in the close-knit Amana communities of earlier times. Quilter Susie Hostetler is safeguarding a tradition, a way of life in the Amish communities. Russ and Jackie Leckband are holding onto the simple customs of the Quaker communities. Pam Dyer Walters and Donna Wood, totally self-taught, simply create but within the influence of Iowa. Anne Sedars, now retired, took an Iowa product that she knew well, cornhusks, and glamorized it. While potter Bob Andersen incorporates the components of Iowa into his pottery, potter Russ Leckband makes nineteenth-century-style pottery. Sarah Grant-Hutchison and Jim Lueders' wooden creations are not folk art in the true sense. Sarah is a sophisticated, trained artist, but the pieces have a primitive essence to them through the influence of Lueders, who is not formally trained. Their works are distinctly Iowan.

I realize I wrote this book so I could get to know these close-to-the-earth artists and learn more about my roots, my heritage. I left Iowa thirty years ago, but keep coming back again and again to this special land and the people who regularly look to the sky to analyze the weather for their livelihood, and the people who care about preserving remnants from the past and who care about their neighbors in a rare, old-world way.

IOWA FOLK ARTISTS

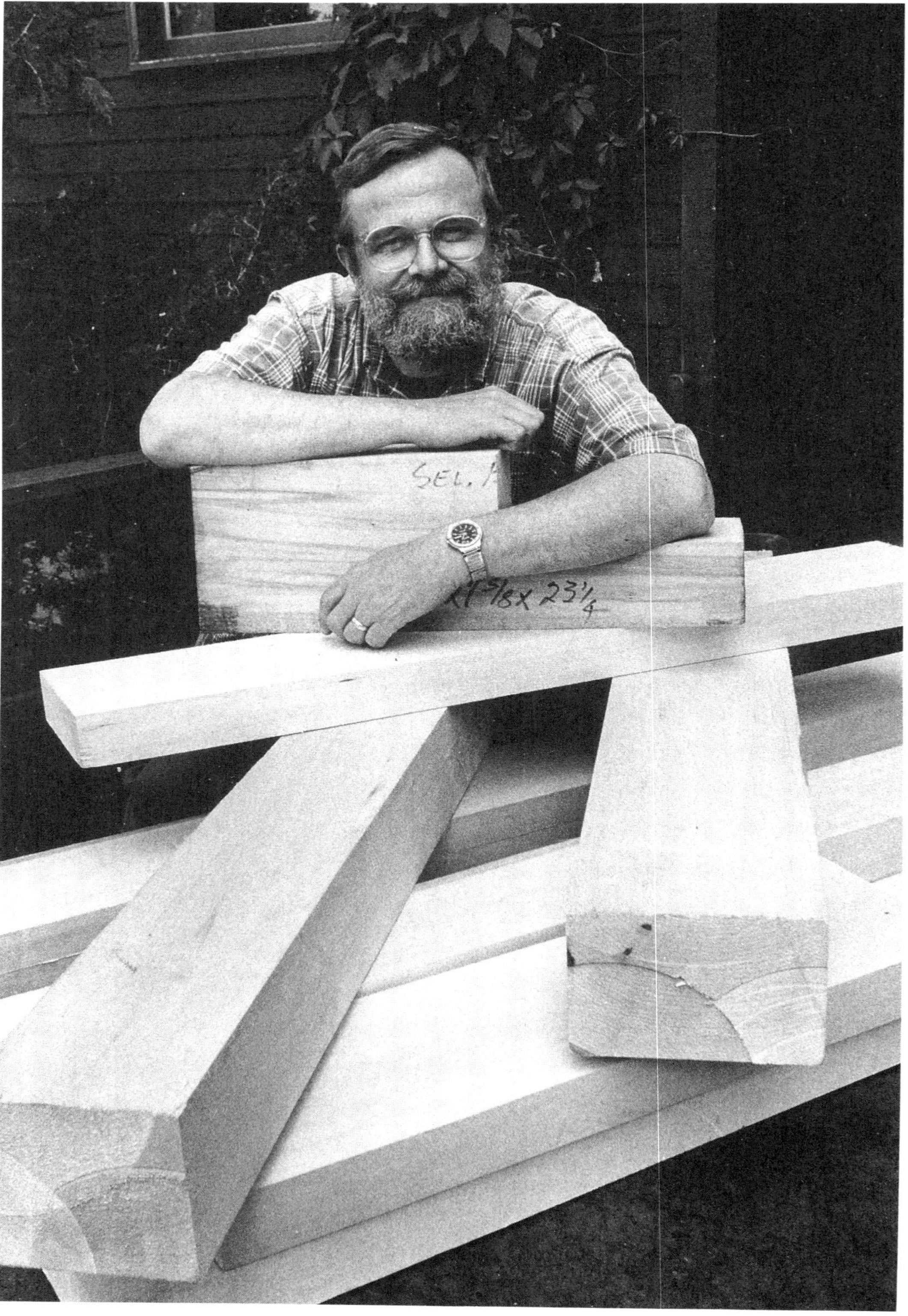

SEL.
X 9/8 X 23 1/4

HARLEY REFSAL

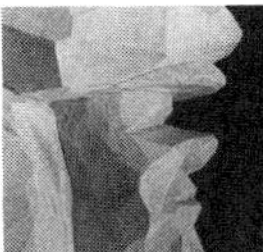 When King Olaf V of Norway visited Iowa in 1987, Norwegian-American carver Harley Refsal was asked by both Decorah's Luther College and the Vesterheim Norwegian-American Museum to create a gift for the king to take back to Norway.

"It was a profound bunch of days," Harley, who has a rugged Scandinavian look, recalls. "I kept thinking it would be so nice to have my grandparents, who emigrated from Norway out of necessity, around. They were poor and to think that only two generations later their grandson would be carving a piece, depicting them, going back to Norway with the king. ... "

So Harley remembered his grandparents in the powerful piece "Taming of the Prairie." The woman, his grandmother, her hair drawn back, is stooped on the barren prairie planting a pine tree. The man, his grandfather, has dug the hole for the tree and stands beside her.

He explains the stark loneliness of the work. "The Midwest prairie was about as different an environment as it could be for them. It was hilly where they came from in Norway. There were mountains and sea and trees all over the place. There was no farmland. Here, they got the good farmland two thousand miles from the sea and no trees."

Harley had empathy for the feelings his grandfather experienced as an immigrant farmer. "My initial contact with things Norwegian stems from my grandparents because my grandfather lived with us when I was a boy. When he died in 1950, he had lived in this country fifty-six years and still spoke only Norwegian. ... I remember how sad my grandfather was. He never was one who enjoyed the move to America. His wife died, and the older he got, the sadder he got that he came to America."

Through his grandfather he learned about the rural immigrant heritage. He learned about nineteenth- and early twentieth-century farm life while growing up on an "all purpose general farm" with hogs, cattle, and crops near Hoffman in southern Minnesota. With these underpinnings he is bringing back Norwegian flat plane carving, a folk art that was almost extinct, not only in the United States but also in Norway. "There is a linkage between what I do now and the way I was

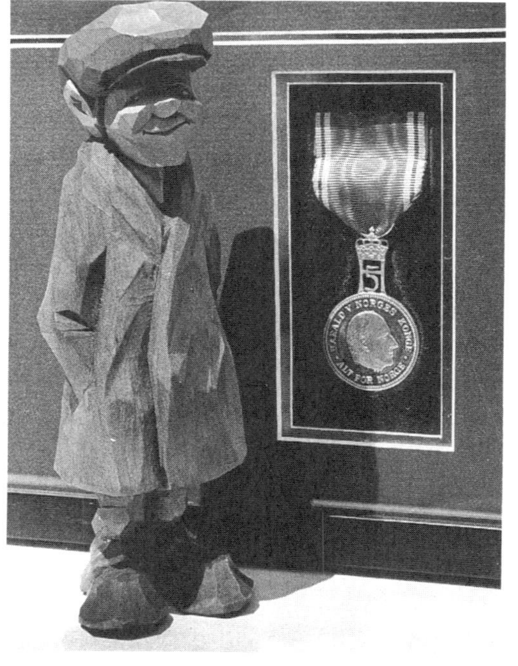

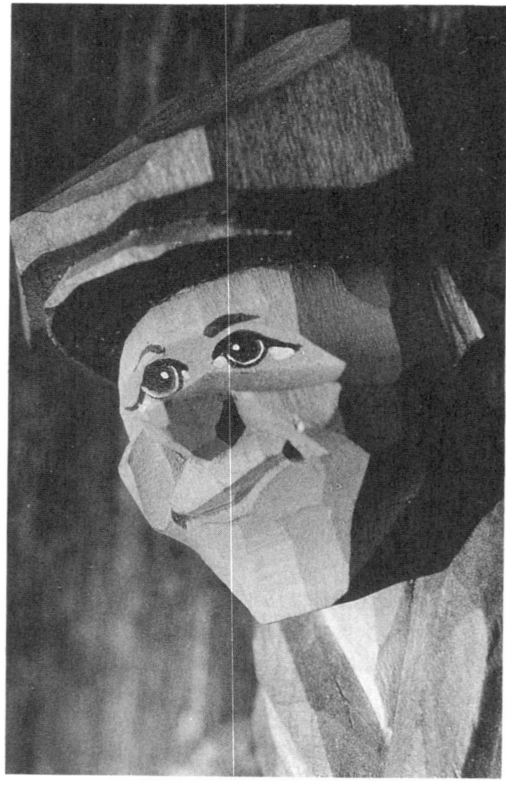

Harley was given the St. Olaf Medal of Norway for his work with folk art.

Close-up of Harley's carving shows the simplicity of his work.

brought up," he notes. "We're products of our past."

For his contributions to Norwegian folk art in Norway and the United States, he has been given the St. Olaf Medal of Norway, awarded by the king and government for contributions to Norway and for the enhancement of the relationship between Norway and other parts of the world. Approximately five medals are conferred each year.

It is Sunday and Refsal, at home in a barn-red clapboard bungalow near the Luther College campus in Decorah, is wearing cargo pants and a loose plaid shirt. Ask him where he carves, and he picks up a sheet from the dining room floor, and on his deck waves it clean. "When I'm done, I come out and give the sheet a shake." In the summer he carves on the deck overlooking the verdant backyard.

Harley, who is self-confident and down-to-earth, was raised in what he calls the old-fashioned way "where we farmed with horses and did things in an inconvenient way." He attended a one-room school with sixteen children, one teacher, and eight grades before transferring to a school in town in third grade. He was constantly reminded of his ethnic roots—he spoke Norwegian at home, ate Norwegian immigrant food, listened to Norwegian songs at funerals and long prayers in Norwegian at mid-week prayer meetings.

As part of this Norwegian heritage, no money was spent for anything unless it was necessary. "It was only spent because it was needed, not because you wanted something." For instance, Harley only had one pair of boots because a second pair wasn't really needed. He spent over an hour on the farm before school every morning cleaning the barn and feeding the animals. "So I wouldn't get laughed at at school, when I came in from the barn and while I ate breakfast, my mother cleaned my boots.

"You tried to cover up the smells. I was acutely aware the farm kids were called barn smellers. If you were a well-to-do farm kid, you had two pairs of boots. I didn't." He is still grateful to his mother for quietly cleaning his boots so many mornings.

On cold mornings his father drove him to school on a manure spreader pulled by a team of horses. "He would have already cleaned the barn and driven into the field," Refsal recalls. "He would have just come back from that. The car would be snowed in, and that (the spreader) was out anyway. I didn't want to touch the edges. It was fresh, and I didn't want to come to school smelling like that."

Instead of rebelling against this upbringing, Harley absorbed it, cherished it like a handed down treasure found in an old trunk. He went to Augsburg College in Minneapolis and studied Norwegian. "I realized it came very quickly. I realized how much old seeds had been planted and taken root."

As a child Harley did some whittling. He still has a tomahawk he carved and shaped out of a peach crate. Sometimes he made toys. "I grew up in an atmosphere where farmers were generalists. The daring to do something with your hands was certainly there. There was always stuff to fix—wagon boxes, barn doors, furniture, calf pens."

In 1967 he made his first trip to Norway with the Augsburg College choir. "I saw for the first time the small wooden figures. I was smitten. What was interesting to me is that they were unrefined, minimalist. I thought this is something I can really relate to. It was love at first sight. You could see the marks of the knife.

"Trying to say a lot with a little is difficult, but I was hooked. I learned the difficult art of simplification. My admiration for the practitioner of that style of carving grew and grew. They'd done it with one single knife."

Figure carving helped him to connect to his own ethnic background. "I was connecting with a little bit of myself. The rural subject matter and understatedness—it was a decent fit."

After Augsburg, he went to the University of Oslo for a year. He returned to the United States and attended Luther Theological Seminary in St. Paul for four years. In his leisure time he carved. By the end of the 1970s, he was starting to sell pieces, and in the 1980s he was getting invitations to teach workshops and classes. During this time he served as chaplain at Luther College and then as head of the international student office. He was also teaching Norwegian.

Meanwhile, on visits to Norway Harley saw fewer of the traditional carvings. He longed to learn more about the art, to know where the tradition came from, to talk to old-time carvers.

To find answers, he needed to spend time in Norway. So in 1988 he took a year's leave of absence from Luther to attend Telemark College in Rauland. To raise money for this year, he and his wife, Norma, sold their Decorah house and car and auctioned their belongings. They went with children Carl and Martin.

In Norway he asked about the old-time carvers. He got the answers "Well, shoot, he died" and "No, he's 92."

"Suddenly there is no one," Harley recalls. "When I asked about it, all sorts of people were doing it, but when I got down to it, they're gone."

During this time the administrators at Telemark College asked if he would teach a weekend class in carving on a trial basis. The class immediately filled with local folks anxious for knowledge about their country's traditional carving.

Harley now teaches classes in Norwegian figure carving and the history behind it at Telemark twice a year. His textbook *Woodcarving in the Scandinavian Style* is the principal carving book used in both Norway and Sweden.

At Luther he instills in Scandinavian students a sense of their culture. "Lots of students are Scandinavian, but for them the language is gone but the interest in the culture is there. They need to learn the culture in a non-language way through folk art."

Not only the Norwegian culture but the harshness of the

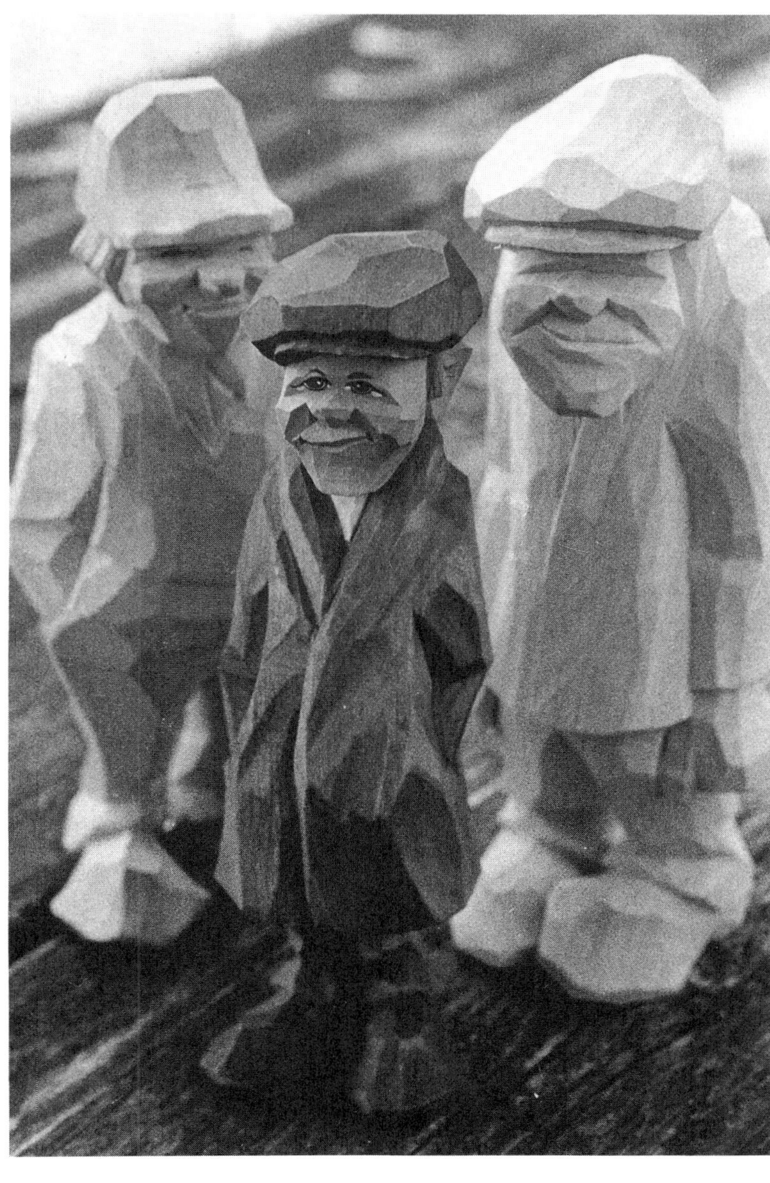

Harley's carvings have distinct character.

early American life comes through in his carvings. "It goes back to farming. That's what I know best—the large, rough, flat surfaces. They go hand in glove with depicting the hard-working, rough-hewn folk.

"When it comes to wood carving, there has been an unconscious sense of being the steward of tradition like my grandfather and father were stewards of the land. The way in which I was brought up informs what I do as a visual artist today."

All of Harley's figures are his own, and, he says, "it's trial and error." "The figures have been my teachers rather than classes." It now takes him about a half-day to carve a figure, but "that's only because I've been carving for thirty years." It once took him several days to carve a figure. He likes to carve timeless subjects, often choosing immigrants.

Basswood is his medium. He saws a rough profile with a handsaw before he takes out his carving knife. He started out using a pocketknife that had been his dad's and added other knives to this. "I started to be taken with the charm more and more of less and less," he remembers.

He unhooks from his belt and holds up his *tollekniv,* a simple Norwegian all-purpose whittling knife, which he made. "If they could do it with this, I can too." He—and sometimes Norma—paints the figures with a thinned acrylic paint. "I want the wood grain to show through," says Harley.

A respect for the passage of time was handed down to Harley and is incorporated into his carving. He likes to think about his grandfather who came to the United States in 1890 and worked four or five years at no salary to work off his passage. "Then he worked a few more years for salary to go back and get my grandmother and bring her back.

"When you think of the whole process taking a decade— that patience showed in handwork. They thought generationally and for the long term rather than the short term—the next quarterly statement." He looks up at the tree next to the house. "If I were a farmer, I'd top a tree, limb it, and put a flat stone over the top to keep the water from coming into the grain—as a repository not for me but for my sons. Then they'd be dried and preserved by creosote in thirty years."

As a contrast he points to new boards used in the repair of gutters on his house. They have split. "Think of that time compared to now when we need to get things done in such a hurry. I can't help but think that the old-fashioned way of being brought up instilled in me the unconscious feeling that the fastest wasn't always the best—that there was some value in passing of tradition onto another generation rather than let it die."

It would have been easy for Harley to follow the family tradition of farming. His father, depressed by the transition of the old agriculture into agribusiness, discouraged him.

An incident when Harley was in ninth grade was poignant in his father's memory—and in Harley's. His father took ninth graders to an agricultural short course. The teacher told them that a calf born in winter "is such an economic liability that one should take a hammer and knock it in the head."

Harley stops ... then continues. "My father was just livid that a teacher should talk about doing that to a living thing. We had a several-hundred-pound hog that we worked on for weeks.

"If you are a steward of the land, you cared for things. When weed spray came in with hesitation he started to use it but didn't have a sprayer. He'd mix it in a barrel and spray it by hand. 'They tell you this is safe,' he said, 'but there's something wrong here.'

"When he was using the tractor, he was plowing into pheasant nests. He couldn't hear where. With horses he had a foot lever that would raise the cutting bar. If a pheasant flew up, he could raise the bar and not destroy the nest.

"Everything changed. For my dad the cultural part of agriculture was what he was interested in. ... It was folk culture."

It had to have been the result of a long-thought-out decision, a painful one, when his father said to him, "As much as I love farming, it's because of that I don't want you to go into farming—not the farming I know today."

But in his carvings Harley is perpetuating the agriculture that was a folk art so anyone who sees them at the Vesterheim Museum in Decorah or Royal Palace in Oslo will not forget an earlier, simpler rural life. "I'm working with different tools, creating different crops than my father and grandfather. But the idea is the same. Using simple materials—low-tech, high-touch. That's how my father farmed, and that's how I carve."

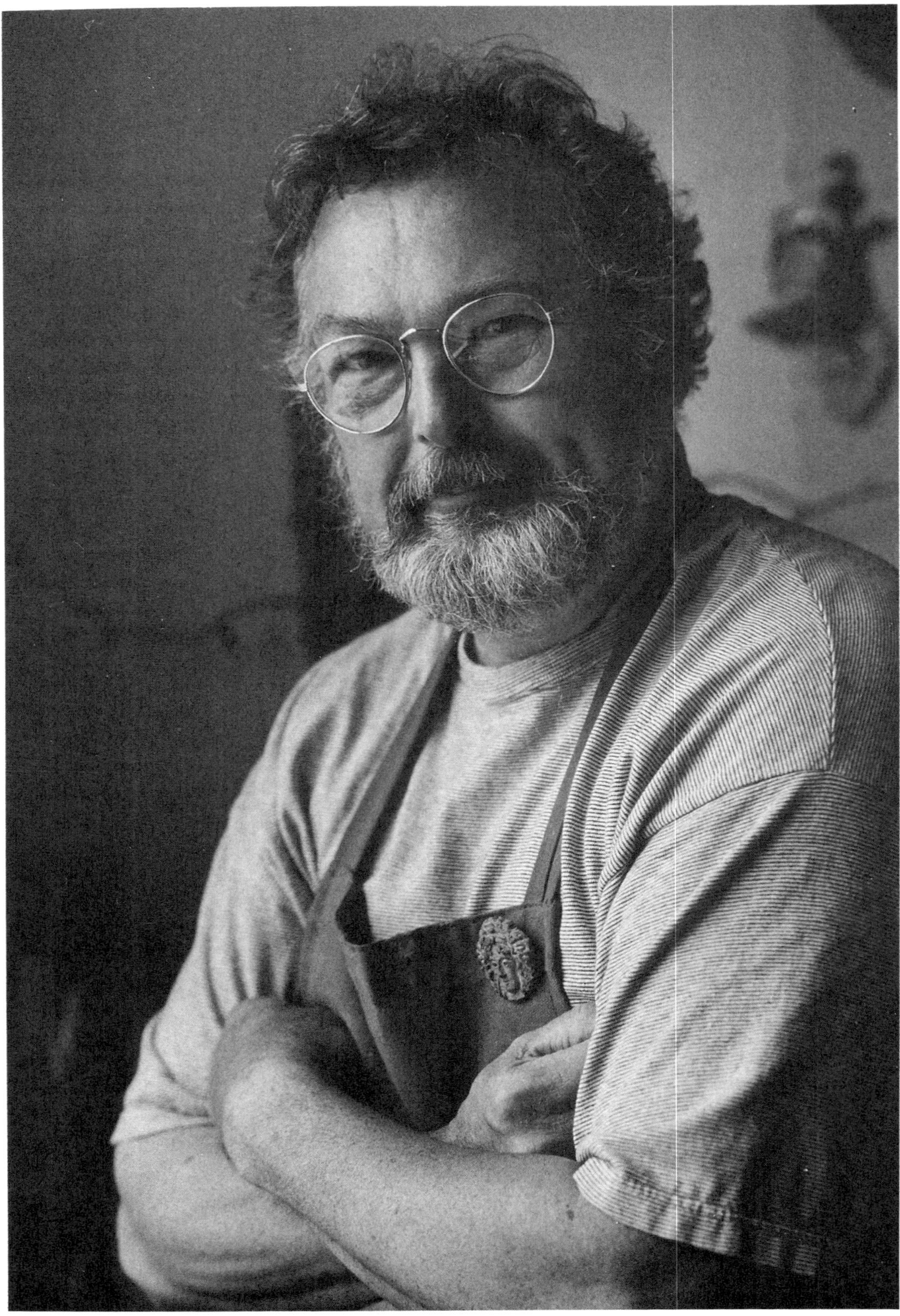

BOB ANDERSEN

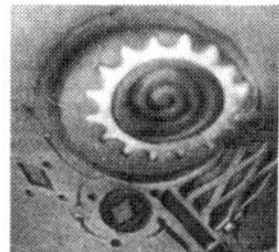

When potter Bob Andersen was growing up in Waterloo, he loved to go to the annual Dairy Cattle Congress with his school class. But he didn't join the throng of classmates headed to the midway. "I went to the animal barns and looked at the cows and beautiful animals."

On Saturdays, instead of shopping with everyone else, he took off for woods near his house. "I'd take my drawing pad to the woods and sketch. I was more interested in being in the woods. I was the fat kid in the corner from junior high on. I always felt different, but that's okay. I learned to accept that."

Bob was studying the components that make up Iowa—the rural elements that make his pottery distinct. "It is of the people, of the land, and of the animals on the land," he explains. "The folk artist draws from his experiences, draws from his environment, and creates new objects. A folk art piece is talking about your life. In this case it's the Midwest life."

Bob is attentively making final cuts on a clay pig that will become a handle on one of the pig casseroles for which he is noted. Wearing a full-length red apron over Bermuda shorts and a shirt, he is standing on a restaurant pad in his pristine studio, just off the square in Pella. On his feet are black tennis shoes and white socks that come halfway up his legs. He ignores time and works with care. It took twenty minutes to throw the casserole. It will take ten to fifteen minutes to press the parts that go on the casserole and an hour to assemble the parts. Glazing will take another half hour because he does lots of painting.

He stops, moves a tray of mugs, and ponders. "I'm one of the oldest surviving, practicing, and working potters in Iowa. People have come to know me and my work." He picks up a cup and starts painting it. "It's a lot of work. Making functional pottery and handcrafted items is a dying thing. The emphasis seems to be toward sculptural pottery and non-functional artwork."

As he throws the pots and molds and carves the pigs, cows, sheep, chickens, and pumpkins that go on the pots, a lot of what is Iowa is going into his work. "Most of the time it's unconscious. I see it when I look at the body of my work at art

Bob Andersen: "My work is known for its distinctive animal handles. This is done by first sculpting the 3-D animal and then making a two-part or one-part mold out of plaster of paris. After the mold has been emptied of the clay original, I can then press clay into the mold to give me many handles. For example, when the clay of the casserole is the same dampness as the clay handle, I can attach the handle to the casserole while it is still damp. The various pieces are about the hardness of cheddar cheese. After the work is dry—two or three days—the pieces are fired in an electric kiln to 1,800 degrees Fahrenheit, the hardness of a red flowerpot. The pieces are then glazed and refired to 2,200 degrees Fahrenheit. This hardens the pottery to a stone-like hardness, hence the name 'stoneware pottery.'"

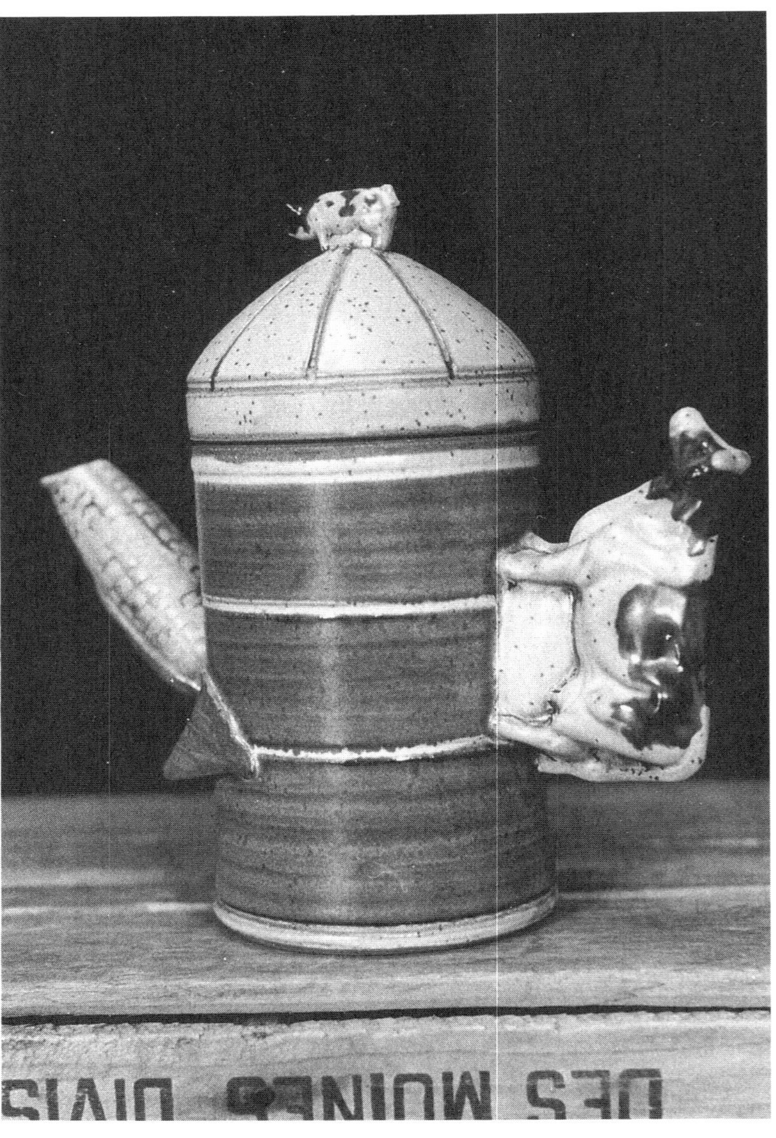

Bob's silo coffeepot incorporates Iowa elements.

fairs. My work doesn't look like anyone else's. I have been influenced by my surroundings, young and old. People come up and tell me great stories about cows, horses, and farms."

The farm animals are handles and knobs on his butter dishes, pitchers, creamers, bread pans, pie plates, and platters. His showstopping coffeepot is in the shape of a silo with a large cow or pig for the handle and corn as the spout. The College of Agriculture at Iowa State University buys his pottery for gifts. His teapots have gone to Russia; his coffee mugs to China.

Recently he sculptured a pickup truck for a coffee mug.

IOWA FOLK ARTISTS

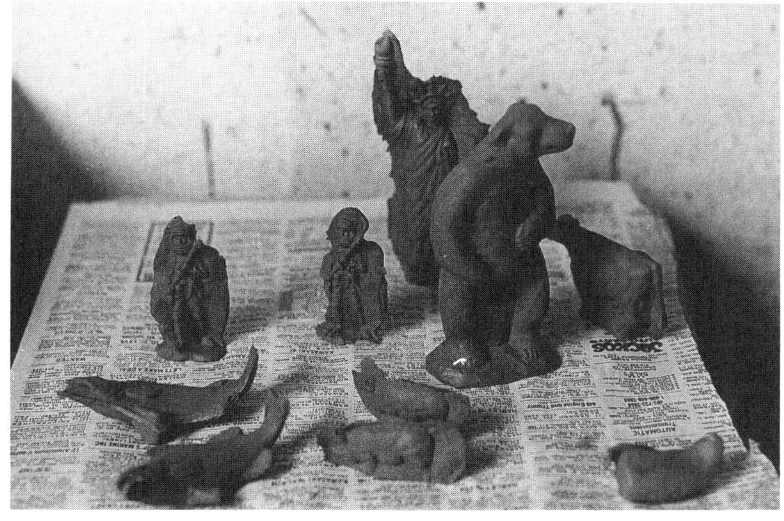

Molded animals to be attached to Bob's pots.

"Pickups and farm animals are pretty much a part of living in Iowa. People would come up and tell me their pickup truck stories. It touched them deeply. One woman told me about a 1948 green truck she had had. Another family told me about their old blue truck.

"I know other craftsmen don't get things like that. They get 'What do you do with this,' not how close this is to the buyer's life."

He told about a German woman coming up to him and saying, "What is there to like about Iowa? I've never been to a place so uninteresting. There are no mountains—no seacoast."

Bob told her his feelings, which are deep, about the state. "Iowa is deeply rich in wonderful subtleties. I'm amazed every time I drive across the state. It's us. I feel very much a part of the earth I stand on."

Along the way he also picked up a fondness for things from the past. "I was always in love with old things," he remembers. "I like the old arts and crafts and the Victorian home."

After high school Bob got a scholarship to the University of Northern Iowa—and returned to barns to draw animals, this time for credit. He graduated in art education in 1968 and taught in junior high and high school in Eddyville and Ames for four years. He then taught ceramics at the Des Moines Art Center.

"I consider that my graduate study. I really learned how to teach the making of pottery, then honed it down into information on how to throw. It's easy to learn how to make pot-

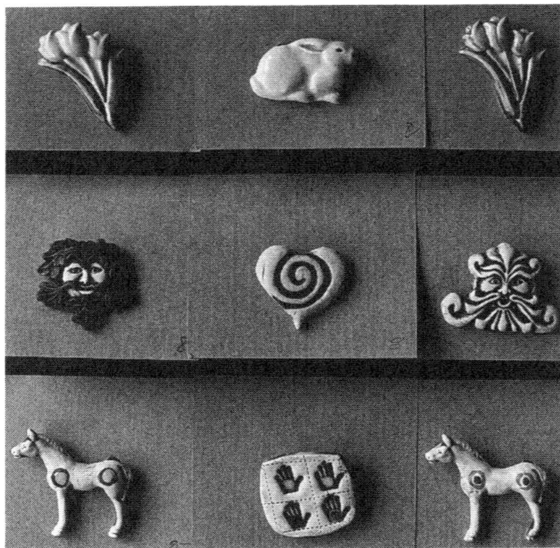

*Pottery pins are part of
Bob's collection.*

*Bob's studio and
shop share space off
the Pella square.*

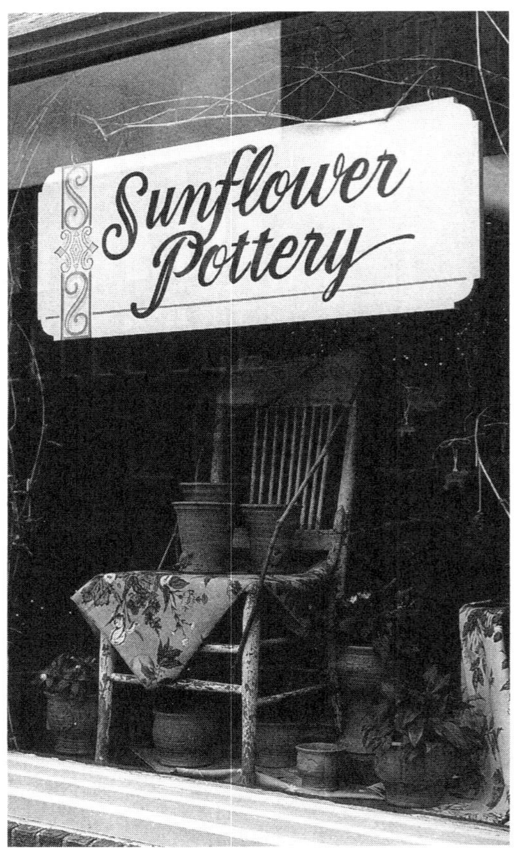

tery. It's hard to have a sense of clay and a feel of clay reflecting your interests."

At that time Bob had to make a choice. Would he go to graduate school or would he start making a living at pottery full-time? "At the art center I knew I could make a living doing pottery. The end result was, if I went back to college, I would teach. Pottery sales were good in the '70s and '80s. Anything you put out on the table took off. If sales were good, there was no reason to go into teaching."

His wife, Connie, whom he met while she was in college, is a by-his-side partner, doing everything except throwing pots. He calls her critic, cheerleader, and best friend. She backed his decision to go out on his own. They lived in Ames until the house they were renting was sold. After looking around central Iowa for a new town, they settled on Pella, the quaint and historic Dutch town that attracts tourists year-round.

They rented a house, then found a studio and adjacent shop on Franklin Street. The studio is not large, but Bob has it

IOWA FOLK ARTISTS

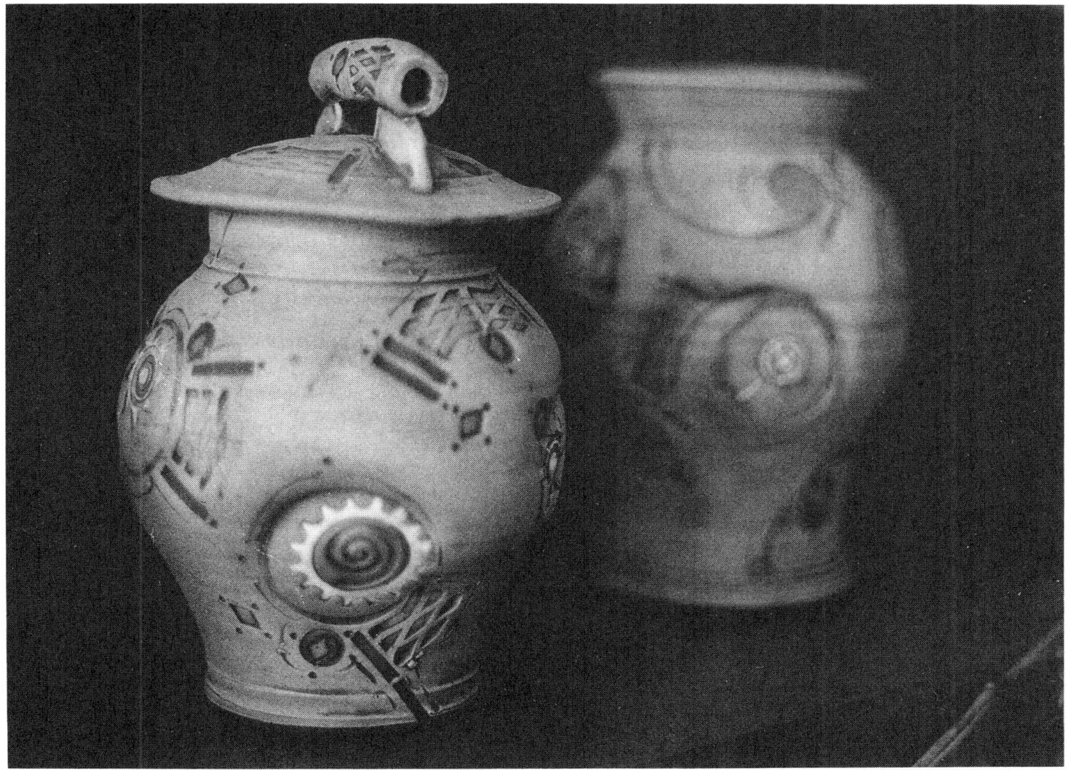

Pot with natural beauty.

arranged so there is room for his kickwheel, two kilns, and shelves for pottery in different stages. They call the business Sunflower Pottery.

Devotion and pride go into each piece of Bob's work. Having a well-crafted piece is important. "There are lots of craftsmen who build up an inventory in the winter. I can't do that. I handle work on each item as individual." He credits his stepfather, who was a builder, with indirectly telling him the importance of patience, perfection. "He didn't teach me, but I picked up from him the idea that you do it right. He built with insulation that was right. He used Pella windows."

He lovingly hand-builds all his mugs, each featuring a farm animal or sometimes a tractor, pickup truck, or pumpkin. He builds each mug around a cardboard tube. Once the clay is rolled out, it takes six minutes to shape.

Today, he sculpted a sheep that adorns the side of a cup and has made a mold from it. He has pressed the clay into it. He gingerly lifts the sheep out of the mold and uses water to stick it onto the side of the cup. Behind him is an inventory of unique molds that he has made through the years.

BOB ANDERSEN   15

He carefully paints each piece where painting is needed. Each piece has two glazes. He makes one of the glazes from wood ashes, something common among Japanese potters. "It's another reflection of my sense of the craft." He fires the pieces for twelve to fourteen hours at temperatures up to 2,260 degrees Fahrenheit, which is mid-range stoneware.

There is no doubt that Bob likes his work. "This is fun to do," he says, accidentally wiping clay into his graying curly hair. "If I'm making a new handle or something new to cook in … what can I do that is more functional or usable or interesting in shape?"

The pottery business is not immune to business cycles, and the 1980s brought the Iowa farm crisis. "There were years when I wished I'd had more pots. Sometimes, I couldn't give them away. In Iowa, if the farm economy is bad, the whole state gets shaky, and we're worrying about our next meal."

Business never picked up again on the art fair circuit, he says. He has watched craftsmen go farther away to sell pots. Other friends make items easy to produce and sell totally wholesale. The Andersens have tried to work the shows closer to home, but they are not as good as they once were. "Our life has been governed by art festivals. Most of the income we've made traveling to art fairs.

"We know we're not going to get rich. I'd like for my wife and I to be comfortable." He stops, looks out the window. "I may have to move out of Iowa. I don't want to leave Iowa. We've done genealogy to know our families are some of the earliest in Iowa. I love the land. I love the change of seasons. I keep thinking about those people in the winter. You have to be tough to live in Iowa. It's not an easy place."

Bob is content with his life and is philosophical. "All my life has been a struggle, but I've never looked at it as a struggle. I've seen people with big, fancy cars wondering what they want to do with their life. I've never thought of myself as successful. I've thought of myself as fortunate. I'm lucky.

"It's not so much being my own boss. I've been fortunate to have found something I can make money doing and really love. That comes for so few people."

The Andersens' children, Erin, Jenna, and Sara, all college graduates who are working in art, actually benefitted from the places art fairs took the family and from helping at these events. "When we went to art fairs, we spent extra time after the fairs shopping, going to parks and museums. They knew how we made a living and the ups and downs. They knew how money came into the house. It was never a mystery. The kids know the only constant is change. There is going to be change in life."

Retirement is something Bob does not foresee experiencing. "I'm not set up to retire," he says. "I plan to die on the potter's wheel. I see most people who retire as waiting to die anyway. They'll have no interests except working in an office or factory. Come sixty-five, they think they'll sit in an easy chair, but they'll lose the spirit of life.

"To work with your hands all your life and to sit down and say you're done working with your hands—it's dangerous."

Yes, the Andersens have worries. "They show up. Is the van going to make the next six hundred miles?" And, he adds, "It's hard to save." There is conversation about a move to a gentler climate, say, North Carolina, and opening a shop. "When I'm sixty-five or seventy, I'm not sure I want to be unloading boxes from the van."

Right now they take time from work to enjoy Iowa's countryside. Early winter mornings, they stop at a restaurant, pick up a simple take-out breakfast, and sit in the brittle cold at Red Rock State Park and watch bald eagles fish. "I have new respect for crows. Some mornings it's 10 below, and we see eagles catching little fish, and the crows are working as far as the eagles."

One of the items that seems to be on Bob's future agenda is seeing his father. He was raised by his grandmother in Iowa City until he was eight and then by his mother and stepfather in Waterloo. He never knew his father and only recently learned who he was. "I understand he loves the land and works with his hands," says Bob.

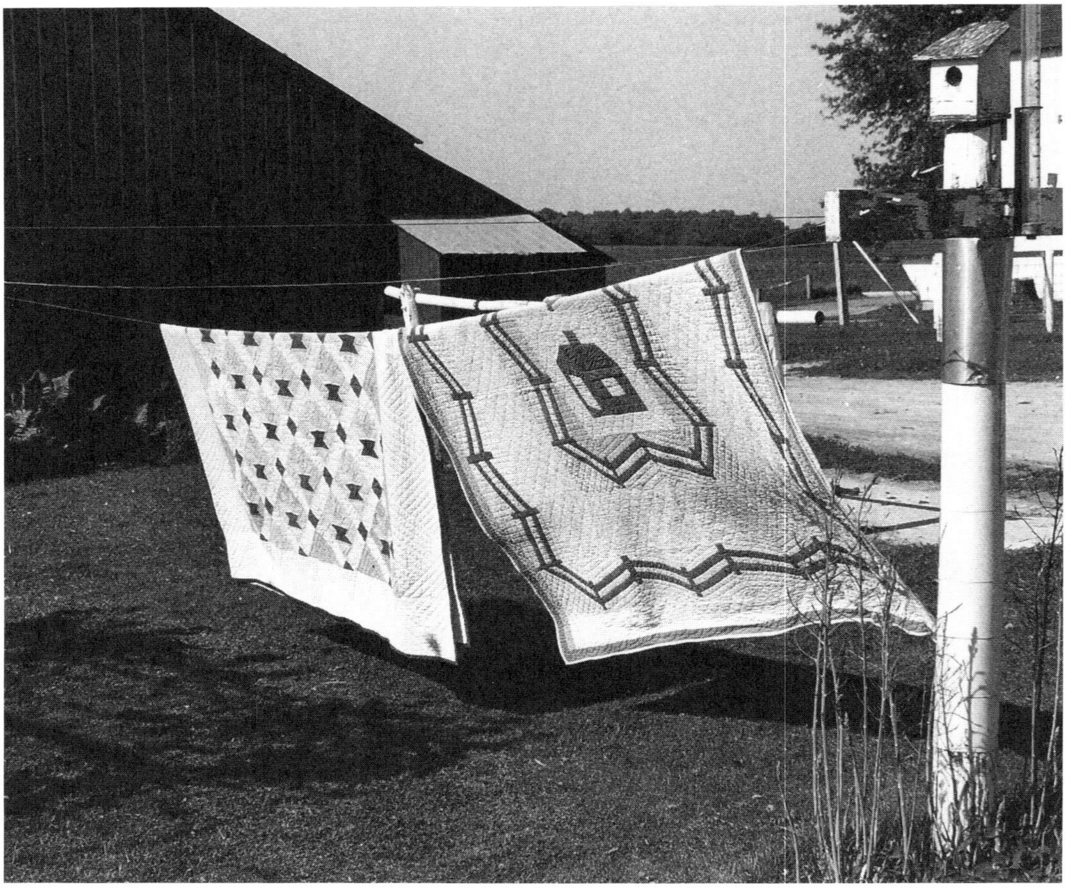

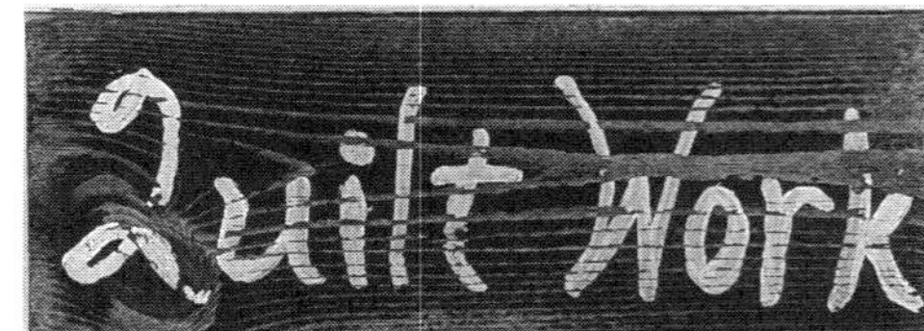
Quilt Work

SUSIE HOSTETLER

It's a Monday morning in early June, and brightly colored clothes rustle on clotheslines in the yards of the big white frame houses on the roads around Fairbank, a remote Amish area in the north-central part of the state. Little boys wearing the distinctive black hats smile through the windows of black buggies drawn by handsome horses.

Down the gravel drive behind a large white house is a neatly kept smaller white house, enveloped by large silver maples. Lettuce and strawberries are up in the garden. Beyond are the straight lines of corn planted in the black soil for which Iowa is noted. The simple black and white sign that used to read "Quilts for Sale" is no longer there.

Susie Hostetler opens the door of the small house. She is wearing a purple dress and white apron. Her white hair, neatly parted in the center and pulled back under a cap, doesn't hint that she was auburn-haired a few years back. She has a classic face with perfect small features and blue eyes. Her complexion does not carry lines that reveal age. Her posture is strong, assertive. When she speaks, her voice is soft, her manner, intelligent.

Her sister, Sarah, who lives in the big white house, rushes to the back door. Susie hurriedly hands her a few clothes. "You have to wash on Monday morning regardless," says Susie. "We're meticulous about it. We press off—iron—a little in the afternoon."

She watches Sarah walk toward the house and comments almost in amazement. "Lots of diapers. They have twins over there," she notes, nodding toward Sarah's clothesline. "She makes all their clothes—even the men's jeans."

Inside Susie's cheerful house the stack of newly made quilts, that months back were piled one on top of each other like bedspreads ready for sale, is gone. She doesn't talk about this or the missing quilt sign. Instead, she takes an early brown and white Abraham Lincoln's cabin quilt from the bed and holds it up. She remembers her mother making it fifty years ago. Today, she offers to sell the quilt for $2,000.

Susie is alone. She doesn't have a nest egg, and she is worrying about the future. "When I came here, I was the only shop. Now there are others, and it's getting commercial," Susie explains. "There are lots of shops going up because we're running out of farms. Young people get married and don't have a farm unless they go to their parents' house and the old people go to the dowdy house, but that only takes care of one child. Young people are going into carpentry, bakeries, and quilt shops."

She has made hundreds of quilts in her lifetime. She emphasizes that she still is in business. Yes, she is experiencing some of the aches and pains of age, but she still makes small quilts. And she cuts and sews larger ones and then "sends them out" for quilting. She orders fabric for quilters. Amish quilts are coveted, and she is proud that hers are in homes not only in the United States but also in other countries.

Susie has lived her life the way she was taught, without letting modernization become a predator. "That's what the Bible says—that we should do as we were taught. Mother used to say that too." She has recorded her life in a diary she has written in daily since she was fourteen.

Susie was taught to quilt long ago on a farm of wheat, oats, and beans near Plain City, Ohio, where she was born and raised. She learned the art at a quilting bee at her family home. "We were all sitting around, and I was taught," she recalls. "I felt pretty dumb."

Quilting is part of the Amish heritage, and she easily learned it. She watched her mother find time to quilt in spite of raising nine children. Her mother made quilts to sell, and she made three quilts to give to each child. "When she died there were enough for each child to have another one," Susie remembers.

This year, she and friends made four quilts for teachers for Christmas. Working twelve-hour days, they accomplished this in two days. "They'd stay for a day, and we had 'carry-in' dinner. Each of us brought a dish." Susie has made quilt tops for her fourteen great-nieces named Susie.

Quilting is still important in the lives of the women in this community, which until recently was off the beaten track for tourists. Many homes have a quilt frame in the living room, and after school young women of all ages sit around it and quilt. "One lady here has three sets of twins, besides others, and quilts. My niece has twelve kids and quilts. It's a recreation. You have to have that too.

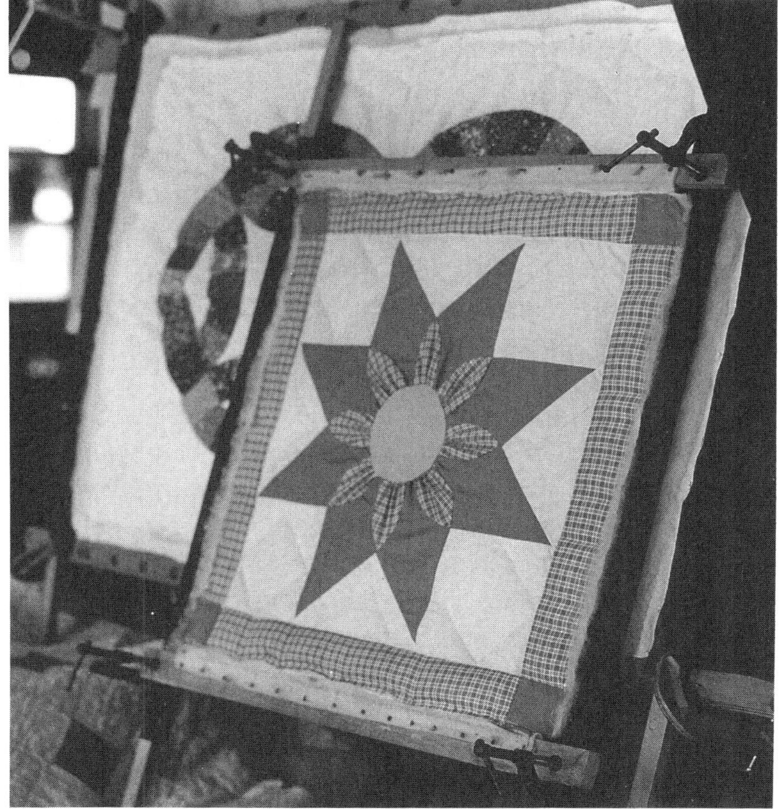

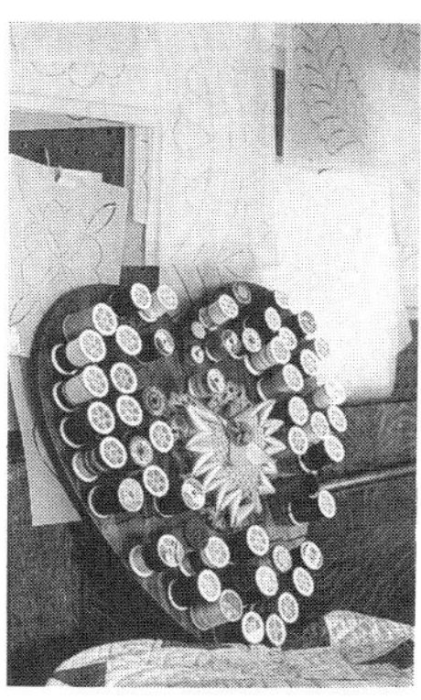

The star dahlia and other quilt pieces laid out in Susie's studio.

Spools of thread for quilting are arranged on a heart at Susie's house.

"They talk about recipes, happenings, cute things the children did, things they are angry about—and," Susie winks, "a little more than they should talk about sometimes."

Susie's favorite patterns are the log cabin, the star dahlia, the schoolhouse, the giant dahlia, and an "old grandma's fan." ("They're doing it new ways.") She remembers her favorite quilt, a giant dahlia in mauves with a light gray background.

She either makes or buys patterns—like the schoolhouse—which she places on the fabric. On a plastic cutting board she cuts around the pattern with a quilt cutter, which is similar to a pizza cutter, to get the pieces. She used to cut the cloth with scissors, which, she explains, Sarah still does, but "this is much quicker."

Once the quilt is pieced together, Susie chooses a plastic templet, which has the outline of a quilting pattern cut through it, allowing her to transfer the pattern. She puts this over the quilt top and pencils through the incision. She makes her stitches along the pencil marks.

For her sewing she uses a treadle machine that she bought in the 1920s. She pumps the treadle with her feet. Sometimes, when her feet hurt, she makes the machine work with her hands.

Ironically, Susie doesn't like 100 percent cotton fabric as much as she likes cotton mixed with some synthetic. "It's easier to work with," she claims. She works with plain-colored fabrics and often incorporates two colors. "We don't even use prints for clothes—just plain colors. We make our own Amish quilts of plain material, but for selling we will put prints in them. Our mothers would have thought it a sin to buy material, cut it up, and sew it together again. They used the pieces left from their other sewing. These are called 'scrap quilts.'"

She is precise with her stitching. Someone gave her a picture of a quilt to be made. She was upset with herself because she was one-fourth inch off in some parts of the quilt.

Susie shows off the cheery sunroom she added to her house. This is her quilting room, where she quilts at a large formica table lighted by sun streaming in through the windows. Beyond are the straight rows of corn.

Susie built the house, and everything about it has been done in good taste, all the while keeping a reverence for the past.

"I live a simple life. It doesn't mean we have to be simple in other aspects—just a plain, simple life. We're peculiar people. I'm living on less and like it more."

This unburdened life means no electricity, telephones, television, or radio. Lamps and a three-burner stove are fueled by kerosene. "Some use wood ranges, but I don't have room in the kitchen." A separate oven is set on burners when she wants to bake. "It's nice for me. I don't have to use big pans."

Outside her home is an icehouse. During the winter blocks of ice are cut from a local pond, put in a wagon, brought to the icehouse, and stored. Throughout the year when she needs ice for her icebox, she gets it from the icehouse.

She saves rainwater to conserve the farm's water supply. "I try to use rainwater for everything I can so they have enough for the hogs. I don't want them to run out of water and think it's Susie's fault."

The house is heated by coal and a wood-fired stove. "I can bank it with coal so it keeps all night." Susie brings in the coal from the washhouse.

In the kitchen are canisters of dried celery, dried egg noodles, and chocolate. She notes that Sarah even makes her own Grapenuts and whole wheat. "We have our own food from the animals. Right now we're eating young fryers. We can meat since there's no way of freezing it. We're not self-sufficient. We still need things from the store."

The living room and dining room floors of her house are beautifully polished narrow-cut oak. In the living room is the leather-covered settee, with low-relief carving on the arms, that belonged to her parents. A handsome rolltop desk sits on one side of the room. Wood box, books, two calendars, and an Amish-made bent hickory rocker complete the cheerful, tidy room.

A one hundred-year-old walnut table with a rich patina that belonged to her grandmother is the focus of the dining room. Susie pulls the drawer out and notes that the knob was put in with a wooden pin. "She did tailoring and cut her fabrics on this," she notes with pride.

Her bedroom has a quilt on the bed, a rag rug on the floor, and a bookshelf with books. She does lots of reading "since we go to bed with the sun." There is a guest bedroom, also furnished simply.

She notes that she has as many household worries as anyone. At present the problem is the wringer. It's broken.

It has been twenty years and two moves for Susie to get from Ohio to Iowa, and she doesn't regret it. When her parents died, she was alone on the farm in Ohio and "didn't like what was happening, and it was getting progressive in the church."

A sister asked her to join her family in Missouri, so she packed up and hired someone to drive a U-haul. She built a house behind her sister's and did housework to pay for it. "I could have taught school, but I decided if I built a house I wanted to live in it."

She was there almost eight years when her sister decided to move out of Missouri. At that point, her other sister, Sarah, said, "Come here." She hopes this is the last move but seems nervous that progress could force her to move again. She points out that farmers in this area still plant, weed, and spray with horses. The harvesting is done in the way threshing used to be done, and the husking is done by hand.

She explains that some Amish in the Fairbank area are leaving, making new settlements. There is a scarcity of farmland in this, one of the best agricultural areas of Iowa. Fathers buy farms to hand down to their sons, but now there are none available. One of Sarah's sons sold his farm here because there are no farms for his sons, Sarah's grandsons. "He went to Augusta, Wisconsin, and is helping his sons buy farms there as they get married."

She mentions that Sarah's son Dan reads a daily newspaper and also farm magazines "on the modern ways of farming. We're bound to get some progress."

She looks away nervously. Her voice fades. "I hope I don't have to move again."

In this area of Iowa she returned to the life that was slipping away in Ohio. "There has been a big change in Ohio where I lived with their combines and modern ways. Here they do like when I grew up in Ohio. I've come back to my childhood ways."

Those ways included more than quilting. Susie likes to remember the life she knew as a child—before "progress." There were seven girls and two boys in the family, "so the girls had to pitch in.

"I helped to cut oats and wheat and to drive the team for putting up hay. Mother used to say wheat was too heavy for girls to handle. But we could shock oats."

She cherishes memories of this Ohio where neighbors helped each other whether threshing or making quilts. "Dad had a threshing machine, and he had a threshing ring—a dozen men who helped. They'd go from one farm to the other and help men with threshing of oats and wheat. They'd finish and settle up with each other. They'd pay each other. If they'd done a farm that didn't need much threshing, they'd pay him because he helped all the others. Then they'd have an ice cream social."

She likes the Fairbank area of Iowa because "our people still like to take care of our own like the Bible says." Recently a neighbor's barn was hit by lightning and "everyone went over and helped."

That the schoolhouse pattern shows up in so many of Susie's quilts and hangings may not be coincidental. She taught school in one-room schoolhouses in Ohio and Indiana for thirty years, often walking a fourth mile on a back road in snow up to her knees.

"I tried to serve my church doing that. I felt a responsibility to educate and to help the children to help themselves to make something out of their lives."

Her biggest problem was discipline. "They would try you until they knew the score." Many of the children she taught still spoke what she calls Pennsylvania Dutch; they hadn't learned English.

Susie reads the Bible daily. Every two weeks she attends the Amish church. "Here they're more strict than in many places."

Christmas is important to Susie and, because Sarah has nine children and sixty grandchildren, Susie celebrates at her own home. "I always have a turkey dinner and someone over. Last Christmas I had two cousins." She made sage dressing with celery and onions, mashed and sweet potatoes and gravy, cranberries, mince pie, and fruitcake.

At this juncture in her life Susie is doing a lot of thinking about the life she has lived. Her life has been full. She has traveled in most of the states. She has taught children. She has made quilts that are being enjoyed around the world.

"Oh, yes, I've been lonely. I like to be alone sometimes and need to be alone to think and meditate sometimes."

She talks about a letter from a friend in Tasmania who wrote to her, "Our society has much to be desired these days."

"Both societies are losing out," remarks Susie.

When she talks about her future, Susie does not go beyond three years. "I've had my own life to live, and I've tried to make it count."

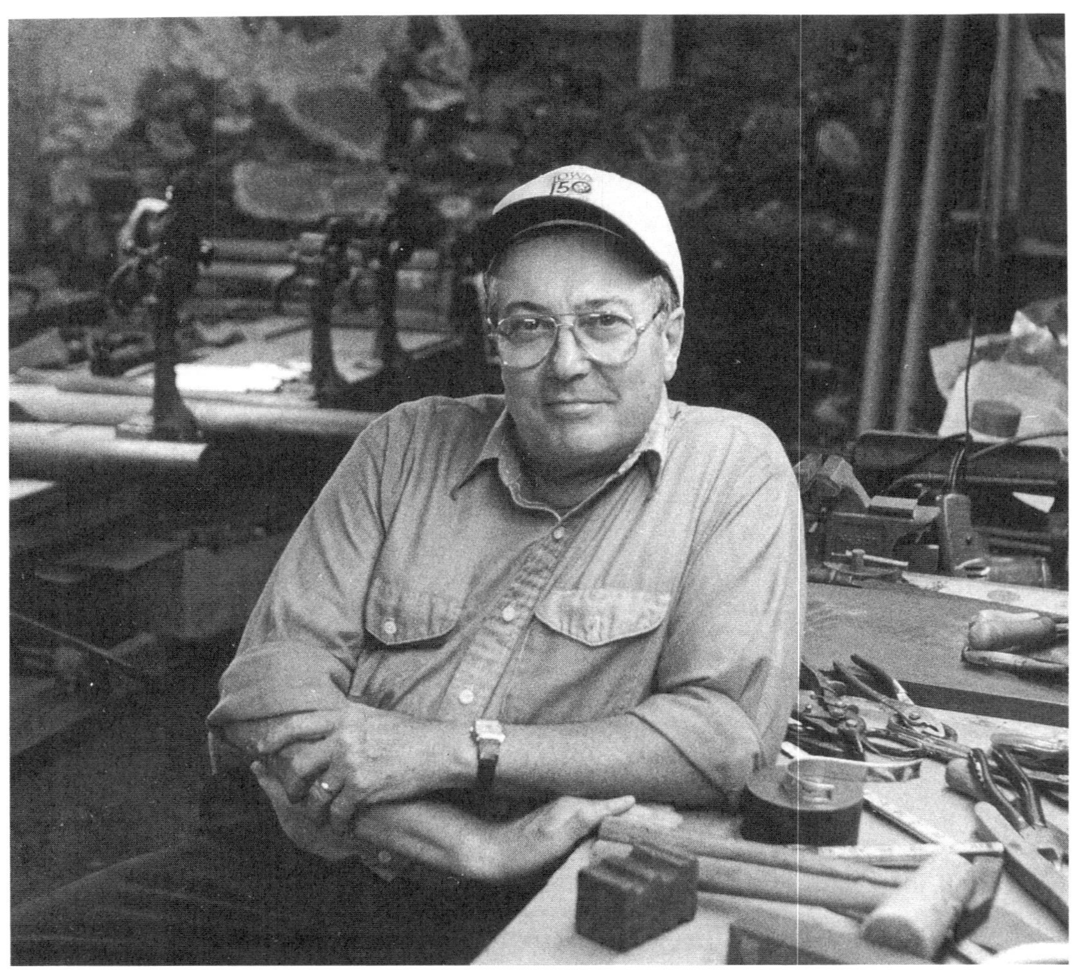

Bill Metz: "Techniques used are the same as those used at the turn of the century. Hand-operated machines, along with a variety of forming stakes, are used to shape, form, and cut materials, all with your hands."

BILL METZ

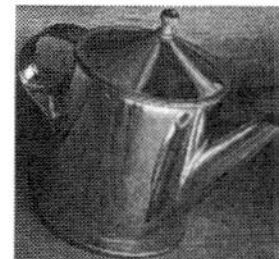

Tinsmith Bill Metz was born in 1933, a year after the Great Change, when the seven villages of the Amana Colonies voted to dissolve the communal way of life and enter the free-enterprise system. He was born in the large brick house where he has always lived on the main road through Middle Amana.

He grew up during years so close to the dramatic change in the Amana Colonies that he had a familiarity with earlier times as if he had experienced them. "The system was not changed overnight," he says, revealing his slight German accent. "It took a period of years to go away until things were modernized. Electricity was not in until 1937. We still used kerosene lights and wood stoves." Milk was delivered from the dairy by horse and buggy. There was no running hot water. Gardens were spaded by hand.

As a young boy he was told stories of earlier days in the villages by his grandmother, mother, and father. "They told us what they'd have to do. Church was important. They attended church eleven times a week. They had their own games as kids. The women learned to knit."

He knew the history of his house, which was built in 1868 by people in the Amana Colonies. It had been a communal kitchen, and his grandmother, Mrs. Fred Hahn, who bought the house after the Great Change, had been in charge. She organized and planned the meals with the help of three or four workers. Because of this, she had high social stature and was given the opportunity to buy the historic house.

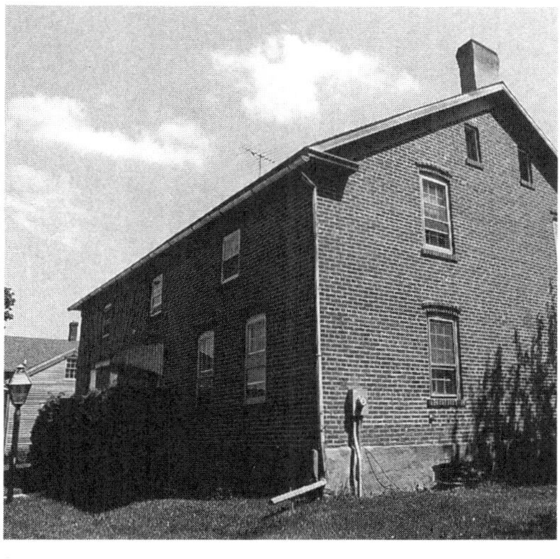

Bill was born in this house, which was once a communal kitchen.

"This kitchen would serve thirty to forty-five people every day, three meals a day," Bill says. "None of the homes had a kitchen. They were assigned a kitchen to eat in. That's where you went morning, noon, and night."

The utensils used in the communal kitchen were made and repaired by Amana tinsmiths. Bill remembers the kallone Kassel (gallon pails) and traditional bunny cookie cutters. "They

were all around." He picked up a familiarity, an appreciation
of items like the tin communal food basket. "If someone could-
n't eat at the communal kitchen, they took the basket home,"
he points out.

He heard how the governing elders of the church assigned
men to occupations—bookbinder, blacksmith, carpenter, basketmaker. "Often the occupations were handed down one
generation to the next. They were self-supporting. Whatever
they needed to be self-sufficient, they had."

He also watched while the basketmakers, furniture makers,
weavers, and harness makers died, leaving no apprentices to
continue their crafts. The end of the communal system meant
the end of the communal kitchen and, ultimately, the end of
the craft of tinsmithing in the Amana Colonies.

The work ethic and the need to contribute to making a better society was ingrained in him while growing up in Middle
Amana. "We learned how to work. We had to work out of
necessity. A few chores around the home had to be done like
filling the wood box. The farm people would pile two or three
cords of wood in the front yard. Then they'd come with a tractor and saw it. Then we'd split it and carry it to the shed."

An old cast-iron kettle was heated over the wood-fired brick
boiler in the backyard. "Mother started a fire for water. All we
had to do was pump water. We'd carry the five-gallon bucket
into the house and pour it into an old-fashioned bathtub."

After Bill graduated from high school, he went to work at a
local plumbing and heating shop. He got involved in the
sheetmetal part of the business, liked it, and ultimately
became a sheetmetal worker. He also developed a keen interest in the history of the Colonies.

His interest in history, his respect for tradition, and his
belief in hard work merged, and in 1980 he revived tinsmithing in the Amana Colonies. "I cheat a little at this hobby," he says modestly. "I'm a retired sheetmetal worker by
trade." He is also an unsung hero for perpetuating a folk art
that was so important to those who were part of the seventy-
seven-year-old communal system in the Amana Colonies.

Bill, dressed for the workshop in comfortable clothes, is
congenial, yet quietly serious. He obviously works hard, never
wasting a minute. The hint of a German inflection when he
speaks is surprising. Yet it reveals that he is connected to "old"
Amana, that his heritage is cherished. His wife, Audrey, who

is from nearby Center Point, is small, outgoing, and intelligent. Pointing out the antiques in the house, she obviously cares about the Amana Colonies and their history as if she had been born there.

His tools—mallets, hammers, pliers—are in the old-world workshop in the basement of the large house. The wood stairs have a deep path worn into them. The floor is dirt; the foundation walls the sandstone of the area. He does his work with the non-electric machines—"used in the trade of yesteryear"—which he has collected through the years.

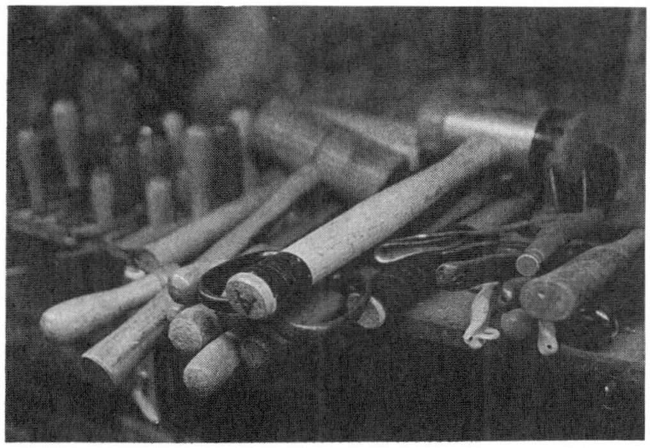

Old mallets and other tools are used by Bill to make tinware.

The strong, old-looking steel machines are lined up in the middle of the room. "For something as simple as a pail, I have to use seven or eight machines to make it," he says. "Each machine has its own function to do."

To make a pail he uses tin plate, black iron coated with tin, which is thin and pliable. He takes the pattern that he has developed, traces it on the tin, and cuts it out with tin shears. He uses a bar folder to hem over the two end edges of the sheet so there is a hook effect when the edges are brought together. To get this hook, each edge is turned but in opposite directions.

A slip roller rolls the sheet into a cylinder and fits the two hooks together. Then a grooving tool fits across the fitted hem and locks it into place so it can't come apart.

A burring machine turns the bottom edges out so the pail is ready for the round disc that will be the bottom of the pail. Then Bill cuts the round disc, turns the edge up, and fits it over the bottom of the pail. With a hammer he fastens the round disc to the bottom of the pail. He finishes the pail with a mallet.

Bill, who cares for his machines like someone might care for an antique car, has found some at flea markets. Friends have discovered others for him, but finding them is not easy. "I think I have four pieces used in the communal system," he says. "There's no proof—just conversation handed down and handed down." The ones he believes are from old Amana include a slip roller, bar folder, and two turning machines.

He finds it difficult to find machines intact. "A number of them have only bits and pieces. Usually something is missing."

Bill makes all of his own patterns—he revitalizes patterns—

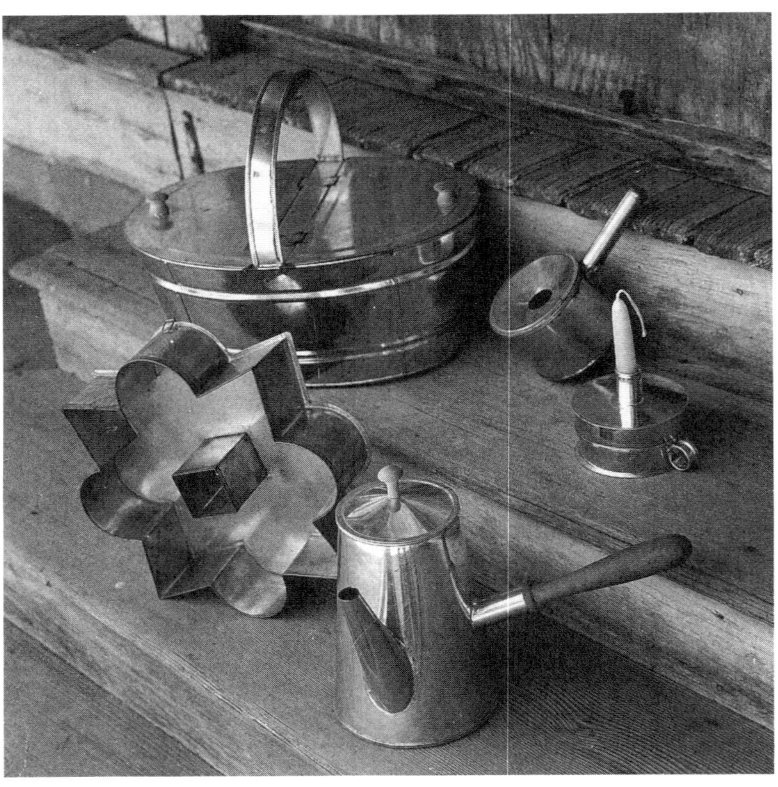

since he can't find any old ones. "Patterns were destroyed when tin shops closed up. They were laid off in a corner, and someone didn't know what they were, and little by little they were thrown out."

For him the most difficult process is visualizing how something will look when drawing a pattern. "The fact that you have to be able to visualize in your mind what you want to make—that you have to know how to prepare yourself for it. ... Lots of times there are intricacies in different seams and different ways to turn the metal."

One of the pieces he has brought back is the elaborate old star-shaped wedding cake mold. "I had one I could work with from the community. I borrowed it, took the measurements, and went from there. I had to sit down and figure out how to go about it and what I'd have to do to get it done." He is now researching the mold, trying to learn the origin of its shape. He suspects that it may have religious significance.

With the molds Audrey makes the Stern Kuche (Colony Marble Cake) recipe that has been handed down with the molds. The cake has four different-colored batters. "The only time it was ever used was for weddings and special occasions," Bill notes. She also makes the bunny cookies.

Through the years Bill has collected the everyday tin pieces made by the old Amana tinsmiths. He picks up an old spittoon. "The elders took these with them when they went to church. They put them under their seats. When they left church, they carried them back home." The cookie cutters he makes are copies of old Amana ones he has found in different homes.

His works are sold by word of mouth, but they are in such demand that he can't keep up. "It's still a hobby, but I think it gets a little out of hand." His best-sellers are the yard lights, cookie cutters, and cake pans. He numbers the yard lights and cake pans and keeps the names and addresses of everyone who has them. He has made about 195 yard lights.

It is obvious he cares about his work, and he wants to know who is enjoying it. "Yeah, you take a little pride," he says. "Yard lights have gone to fourteen different states."

In 1996 he was a participant in the thirtieth anniversary Festival of American Folk Life at the Smithsonian Institution Center for Folklife Programs and Cultural Studies. He credits the Amana Arts Guild with encouraging his hobby and occasionally participates in workshops there. He speaks like a

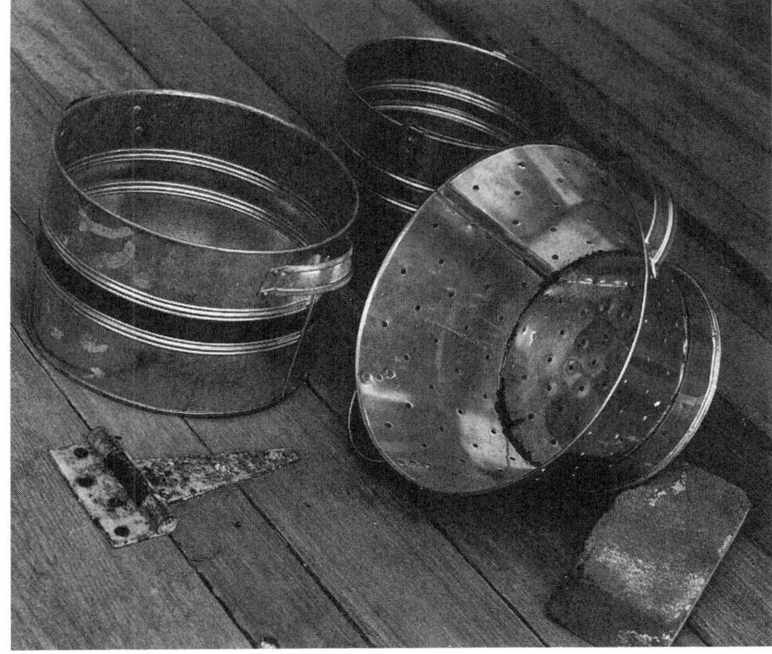

Traditional Amana colander and buckets made by Bill.

master. "They think they're going to learn it in five minutes, and they're not."

Although he works hard at his retirement "hobby," he likes the freedom that comes with it. "The nice part is you can stop and start when you want. I may not come down here at all. I may come all day. Once in awhile I've promised something to someone and have to get it done."

While Bill revives old tinware patterns and molds tin into old cups, coffeepots, communal baskets, and colanders, another kind of change is taking place in the community he has lived in for sixty-four years. Next door a pizza restaurant has replaced the general store where he and his family shopped through the years. Down the road is the giant Amana refrigeration plant.

"Agriculture was important in the Amanas from day one. We've been around it all our lives. It's changing when people don't know how to plant corn anymore," he notes.

Bill's lifetime of remembrances of how things were nourishes his folk art. When he was growing up, German was spoken in the home. "I always tell everyone I learned a second language, but mine was English. I've had to use English the last forty years with my wife being around," he says with a smile. Audrey doesn't speak German, so he used to talk to his parents in German if he was alone and in English if she was along.

There was a time thirty-five years ago when four generations lived in the house—Bill and Audrey, their two children, and his grandmother, mother, and father. Each generation had an entrance to the house. Now Bill and Audrey talk fleetingly about the house being too large—about selling it.

They look around the large rooms and see the old Amana cupboards set against the walls. Old tinware hangs from the walls too. In the hall is an old, thick, bottle-shaped baseball bat that belonged to Bill's father, who was a noted Amana baseball player.

Bill was given that love of baseball and for over twenty-five years has umpired high school baseball and softball in the area. "I got off work at three, changed clothes, and cleaned up. Then I'd umpire from five to ten. There were usually two games. It'd be 10:30 or eleven by the time I got home and cleaned up. I went to bed at 12:30, and at 4:30 the next morning I'd be up again.

"You have to enjoy doing it. It's fun being around kids. This may be my last year. ..."

In the steep backyard that overlooks the Mill Race, he remembers his mother's garden that went all the way down the hill. "We don't eat enough from the garden to put in all that work," says Audrey.

More memories fade in. Bill and Audrey stop by the grape arbor. "This is one of the few houses left with grapevines," he points out. "By midsummer the whole side of the house will be covered with grapevines. They act as air-conditioning. It's a heartwarming experience to live in the same house. You're here so long you don't think about it."

He stops, looks around the yard as if he's remembering sliding down the hill on his wooden sled. "We've got plenty of memories."

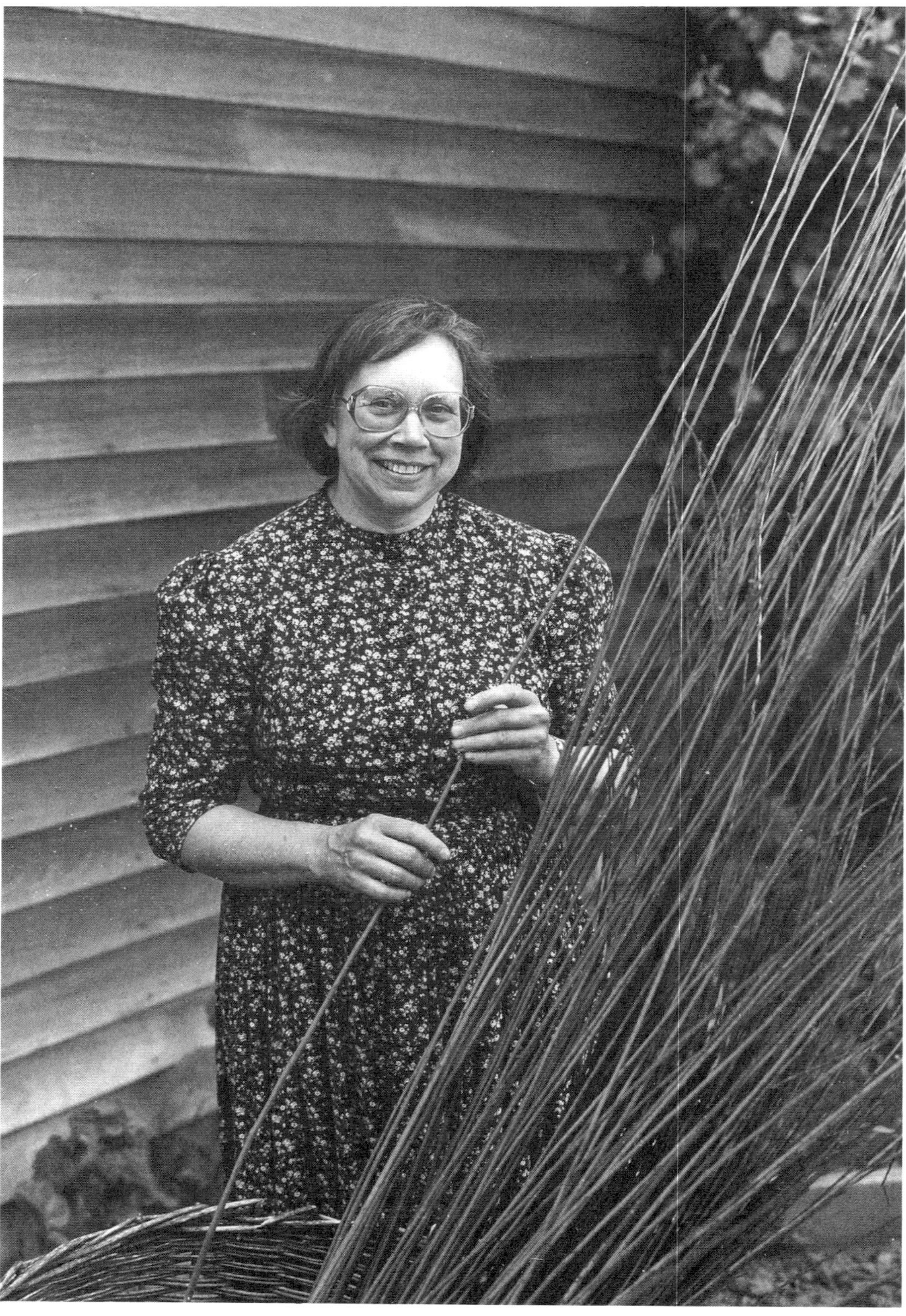

JOANNA SCHANZ

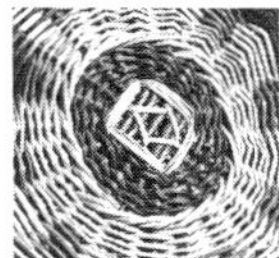 In the Amana Colonies, where heritage, culture, and tradition are cherished like an old photograph album, Joanna Schanz, once an "outsider," is one of the caretakers of the threads reaching back to the community's early days.

She sits in the backyard of the 135-year-old house in picturesque West Amana, a quiet village that has been bypassed by commercialism. The house is on a hill overlooking the verdant Iowa River valley. It has been home to family of her husband, Norman, for four generations since 1932, the year the villages voted to dissolve the religious communal way of life in favor of the free-enterprise system. The house, a rooming house when the Colonies were a religious commune, was built with sandstone from a nearby quarry.

It's as if Joanna has lived forever in this house, in this village where children are told to be home when the streetlights go on. Joanna grew up in nearby Cedar Rapids and didn't know anything about the Amana Colonies "except that they were a place to eat." She met Norman while roller-skating, married him at eighteen, and moved to his home in West Amana as a bride. She was considered an outsider.

"At that time Norman's grandmother's generation talked about outsiders. Now, you don't hear about that anymore," she recalls. "I learned if I wanted to make friends, I had to go out and do it. I had to get involved in the community. I couldn't wait for someone to say hello." So Joanna worked in a restaurant, walked her babies around the village, and got involved in school activities.

Joanna brought with her an appreciation for nature, a love of things natural. At that time she never dreamed that she would be responsible for sustaining an "old" Amana craft, that she would be the one to revive and perpetuate the old art of basketmaking.

The art of basketmaking in the Colonies came from Germany with the settlers of the Amana Colonies. In earlier times community members ordered their baskets from the village basketmaker, usually someone who was old or too fragile to do physical work. These baskets, woven from willow, were strong, utilitarian, and an integral part of daily life. They were made for laundry, picnics, kitchens, apples, knitting, and clothespins. There were baby baskets, field baskets, and clothes baskets. Huge baskets were used for wool products at the woolen mills.

Sometimes they were for fun. "When you look at the old baskets, you see where they got creative," Joanna points out. "On Easter and on indoor baskets, they would put a row of color. They got the color from the woolen mills."

Each of the villages had its own willow patches and basketmakers under the communal system. By 1932 all of the basket shops were closed. By 1970 basketmaking had almost disappeared.

Joanna's interest in Amana folk art started with broommaking. When she and Norman were married, they received a broom with instructions on how to use it so it would be long lasting. It was a gift from Philip Graesser, a blind man who lived in West Amana and was one of the last of the traditional broommakers. She and Norman both treasured it, and when Philip no longer made brooms, they bought his broom kicker machine (broommaking machine). In 1972 they opened the Broom and Basket Shop in West Amana, installed the broom kicker machine, and hired retired villagers to make the brooms. They had revived the craft of broommaking.

Now Joanna had a curiosity about basketmaking, so in 1974 she asked Philip Dickel, the last active basketmaker in the Amana Colonies, to tell her about willow baskets. She knew that, under the old communal system when the church elders assigned adult members of the community a craft or occupation, Philip had been designated a bookbinder. But he had learned basketmaking on his own from Carl Kiesling and had made baskets and given them away.

"He came up and helped me plant a willow patch next to the shop. It takes three years before a patch is established. Four years later, Philip came, and we cut the cultured willow and sorted it. He sat and wove a basket. Then he sat me down, and I wove a basket. He did not have any names for any of the weaves he was doing. Everything was in the basket books, but at that time there were not many books at all."

She often thinks about Philip, who in later years worked in the carding department of the Amana Woolen Mill and as a night watchman at the Amana Refrigeration Plant. Joanna will not take the credit for reviving basketmaking in the

Amana Colonies without mentioning Philip Dickel. "I did it with Philip. It probably was destiny to put Philip and me together." He died in 1981.

After Joanna was captivated by the craft in 1974, she started weaving baskets whenever there were free moments and has not stopped. She raised four children, helped to run a shop, and taught and wrote about the craft—all the while weaving baskets. "I enjoy weaving. It feels right. Sundays are weaving days if I don't have to work." In the winter she weaves in the house; in the summer, outdoors. She now numbers her baskets. In the last few years she has made 250 per year.

She weaves with the cultured willow from the patches she has planted around the Amana Colonies and with wild bush willow, which grows heartily along Iowa rivers. She has also planted patches of willow she has imported from England and Belgium.

Stake and strand "is basically the terminology to describe the type of willow baskets I make," she says. "The stakes go up and down, and the strands are what the weavers are.

"Philip taught me baskets are made to be used. They are strong and sturdy." She picks up an old Amana laundry basket and casually pulls off the bottom rim surrounding it, then pushes it back onto the basket. "All of the Amana baskets had removable bottom rims. This rim protects the bottom of the basket, so if there is wear and tear, it can be removed and a new one put on."

Certainly it is the beauty and the sturdiness of the willow that have given these baskets their distinction. Joanna points to a patch of cultured willow growing in her backyard garden that she cherishes as much as other gardeners cherish their heritage roses. This variety is reported to grow to six feet, but, she says, it will grow taller than that. She guesses that she can make three baskets from the patch. "You don't fertilize, and you watch for disease."

Growing and harvesting willow is an art and, like others, takes time. She cuts the willow in the fall when it is dormant and the patch cannot be harmed. She then sorts the willow branches as to length. If they dry out between the time of harvesting and use, she soaks them from one to twelve days in anything from a stock tank to a bathtub.

"What I'm using now is what was grown last year. Willow

is like fine wine. The longer it sits, the nicer it is to work with. It never gets too old." If she is weaving a big basket, she will use the big plants. For smaller baskets, she will use smaller plants.

The cultured willow slips she planted in her backyard are similar to the willow slips the founders of the Amana Colonies brought from Germany to New York to Iowa for basketmaking. Each village had a cultivated willow patch that was harvested and used to make utility baskets. Joanna explains that cultured willow is preferable to wild willow, which grows all over the Middle West, because it has very little pith in the center. There's more wood, and it's stronger.

Joanna says she does not have a favorite willow basket. "It's the one I'm making at the time. I love to find old baskets from someone's old attic and reproduce them, especially if there is something new and unusual in weaving that I haven't seen before."

For her the most difficult willow basket to make is "Remaining Faithful," a dressed up laundry basket. "It has removable bottom rims and willow embellishments on the side that have nothing to do with the structure. It's so time-consuming to put those in, and they don't do anything as far as making the basket better.

"I don't get to weave as much as I want to," says Joanna, who often starts a basket, gets involved in other activities, and finishes it later. When she works at the Broom and Basket Shop, she often weaves or gives demonstrations. She also helps with Schanz Furniture and Refinishing Shop, which she and her husband own. "If we go on a furniture delivery, it's our night out. We go to Cedar Rapids, maybe Iowa City."

Norman's father farmed and worked in the woolen mills. But the love of furniture making seems to have been a gift from his grandfather who was a furniture maker before the communal system dissolved. Norman founded the furniture shop that makes Amana Colony–style furniture from Iowa woods.

There is little doubt that she has loved living in West Amana. "It was neat raising kids in West. If they were ever in trouble, I'd know about it before they got home. Behind the house is a churchyard they used as a playground." Her son used to get on his bike and go to the river and fish.

She likes the consideration that people give to each other in

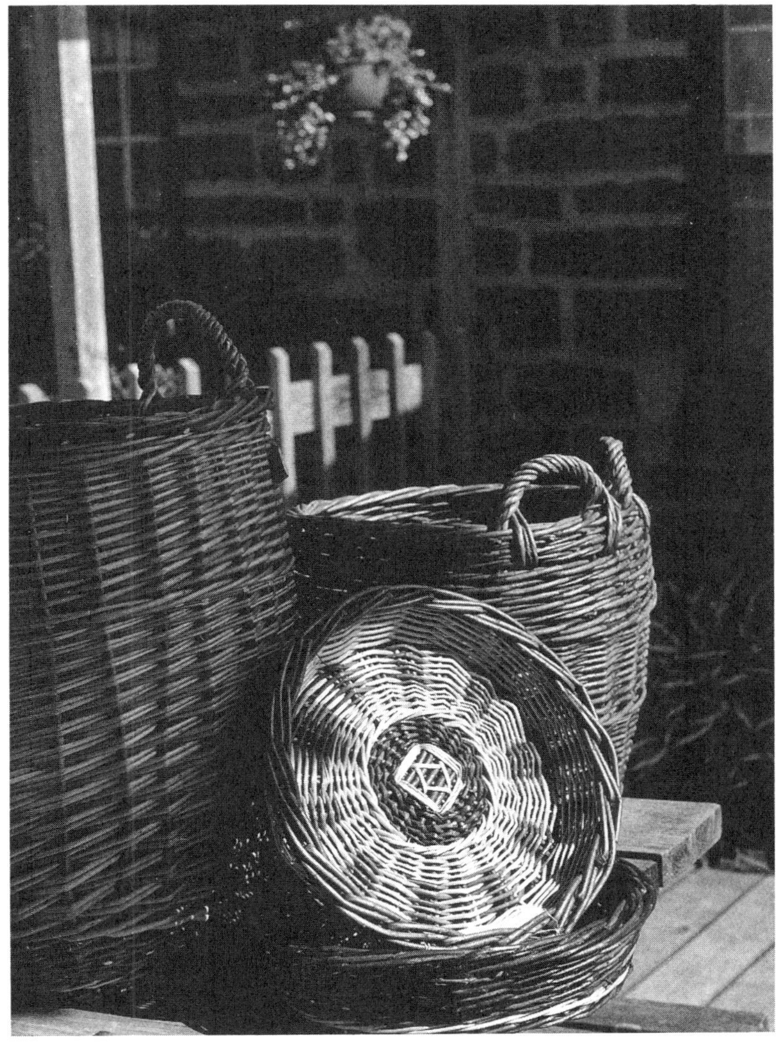

Joanna is perpetuating a historic craft with her handsome baskets: oval laundry basket (left), *traditional applepicker* (back right), *and "off the wall" basket with fancy bottom* (bottom).

such a small town. "There was a blind man [Philip Graesser]. The rule was you don't leave toys and things on the sidewalk."

Jolene, the Schanz's oldest daughter, has a disability and attends special programs. Joanna plans her day to be with Jolene after she is home at four in the afternoon. Joanna has been active in the Association for Retarded Citizens. "The other children learned so much from her. I felt they went out in the world and were kind."

As for basketmaking, Joanna points out frankly, "I'm still learning." She has taken willow-weaving classes in England. She also attended the Corb Market in Lichtenfelds, Germany, an international basket market. She has watched the interest in basketmaking increase since she started the craft. There is

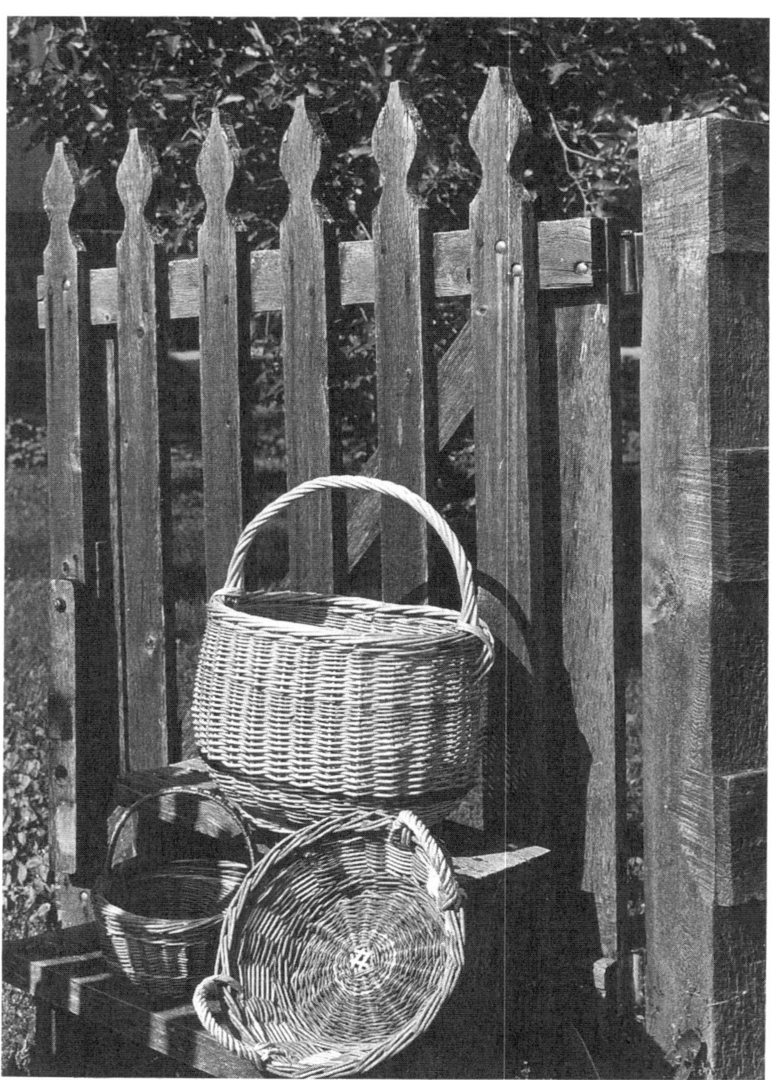

a willow growers network based out of upstate New York. "Those of us who grow willow share information. When you grow willow and make baskets, there's a certain comradery. We're always testing willow. I break away from tradition. If I like what it does, I may change it."

The Amana Arts Guild asked Joanna to teach basketry. And so she taught Laura Kleinmeyer, Kathy Kellenberger, and her daughter-in-law, Michelle Schanz, who are carrying on the craft and handing it down to others. Every February they are involved in Willow Weekend, an intense workshop in the Amana Colonies for those who really want to learn the art of willow basketry. It is set up so that there are four students per

IOWA FOLK ARTISTS

teacher. They bring in willow basket teachers from the United States and abroad.

The baskets these women make are being used in the Amana Colonies today. They are used for laundry, sewing, and wood. They are used as wastebaskets and to carry casseroles to picnics.

All of this fits in with Joanna's interest in the history of the Amana Colonies, where she has spent most of her life. "I'm most interested in the folk art connected with Amana history," she says. "It's down-to-earth, basic survival skills that became folk art today." She wants to make certain that the tradition is perpetuated. "I want to convert more people to basket weaving."

Nowadays, ask old-timers in Amana who the basketmakers are, and they will mention Joanna Schanz. That's quite an achievement for a woman who came to the historic Colonies as a young bride, an "outsider."

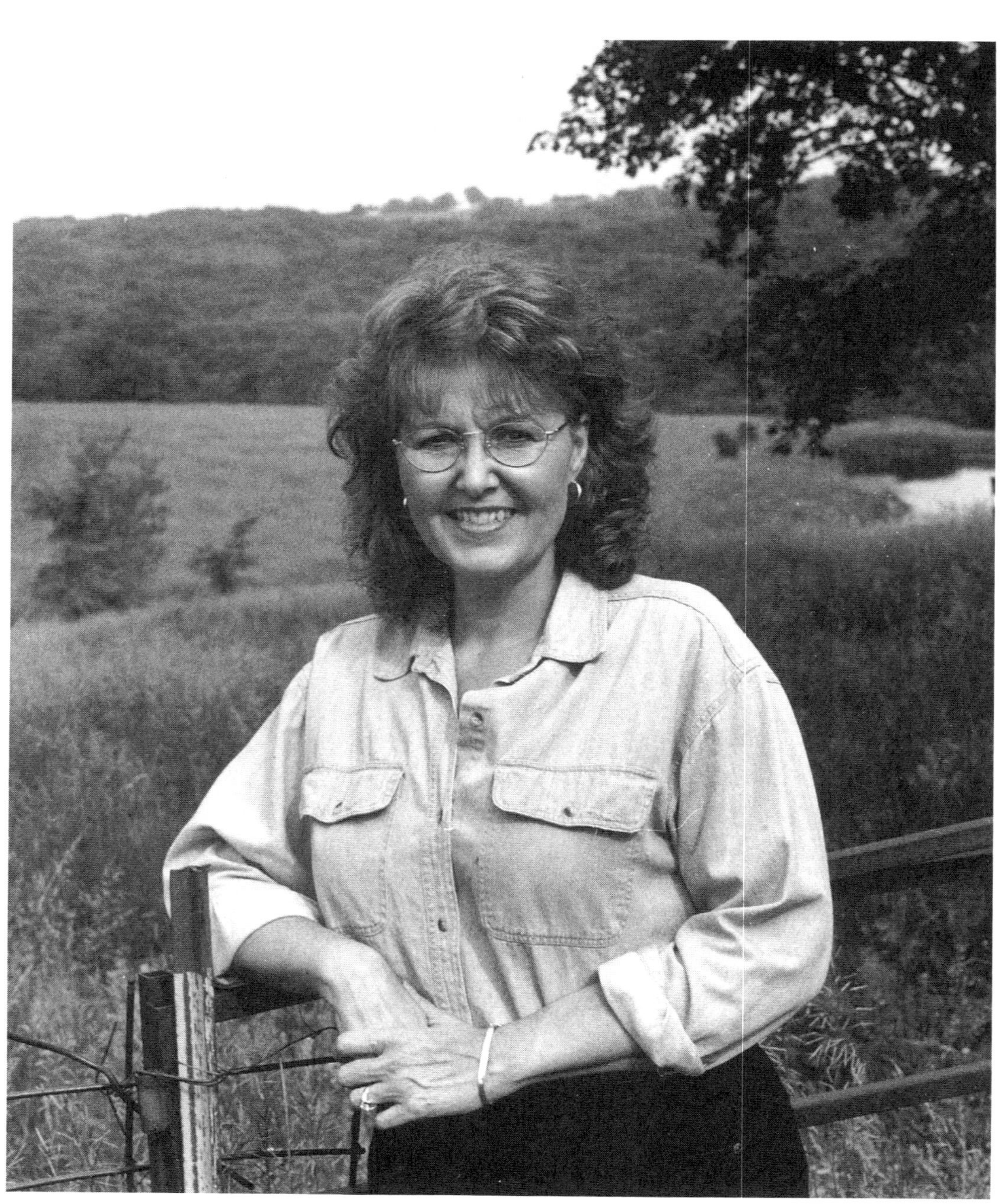

ANNE SEDARS

Anne Sedars: "Using a vegetable dye, I first dye husks. I always work with wet husks. Wrap small [natural-colored] husk around Styrofoam ball for head. Stick wire into ball. Wrap husk around wire for neck. Wrap two cotton balls in husk for bust. Layer husk on top of bust to form bodice. Using lightweight wire, wrap several husks around doll to form waist, apron, and skirt. Glue husk of skirt together. Stuff dry husk under skirt to make it stand out. Glue hair on and any other detail desired. Make bows out of husk for back of apron and for hair."

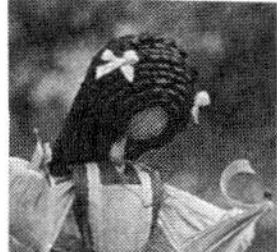

Anne Sedars hunts in the basement of her Prole farmhouse, east of Winterset, for the remains of some folk art she has temporarily put aside. She picks up a cardboard box stuffed with cornhusks, sets it down. She finds the cornhusk Santa that she puts up at Christmas. In another box are three wingless cornhusk angels. Her exquisite cornhusk dolls were in such demand that a folk art she loved became a job she no longer enjoyed.

Her story starts on the farm next door, where she was raised in an old-fashioned way. She walked down a hill one-half mile to pump water. She took baths in a plastic cement mixer from the lumberyard in water heated on the woodstove. Winters, she was up by 5 a.m. because she had to feed the pigs before 6 a.m., when she left for basketball practice. Summers, she threw fifty-pound bales of hay in the fields that her sister picked up with a hay hook and stacked.

One of her treasured memories was gathering eggs at a neighbor's farm. The neighbor made unusual hickory nut dolls. "Each doll had a different expression. She painted the faces, stuffed the bodies, and made the clothes by hand, never using a sewing machine. We'd go in and look. I thought, 'I wish I could learn to make them.' I thought, 'Wow, how can anyone do anything like that?'"

Anne was particularly fascinated by the hair on these enchanting dolls. "She made the hair out of embroidery thread and curled it around a rod."

Thoughts of handmade dolls were tucked away until 1983, after Anne had given up her job as an accountant with the phone company to stay home with her sons, Kelly and Brian. "I moved out here, quit work, didn't know anyone, and thought, 'What am I going to do?'"

She saw someone making dolls from dough and decided to try it. "I thought I had no artistic talent and started mixing dough from flour and salt and making ornaments and figures. I couldn't believe I had the talent to do this."

Later, somewhere, maybe in a magazine, she saw a cornhusk doll. "I thought, 'I can make them.' I wanted to do six dolls depicting each of my sisters." She went to the grocery store and bought a bale of tamale husks. "I started with one

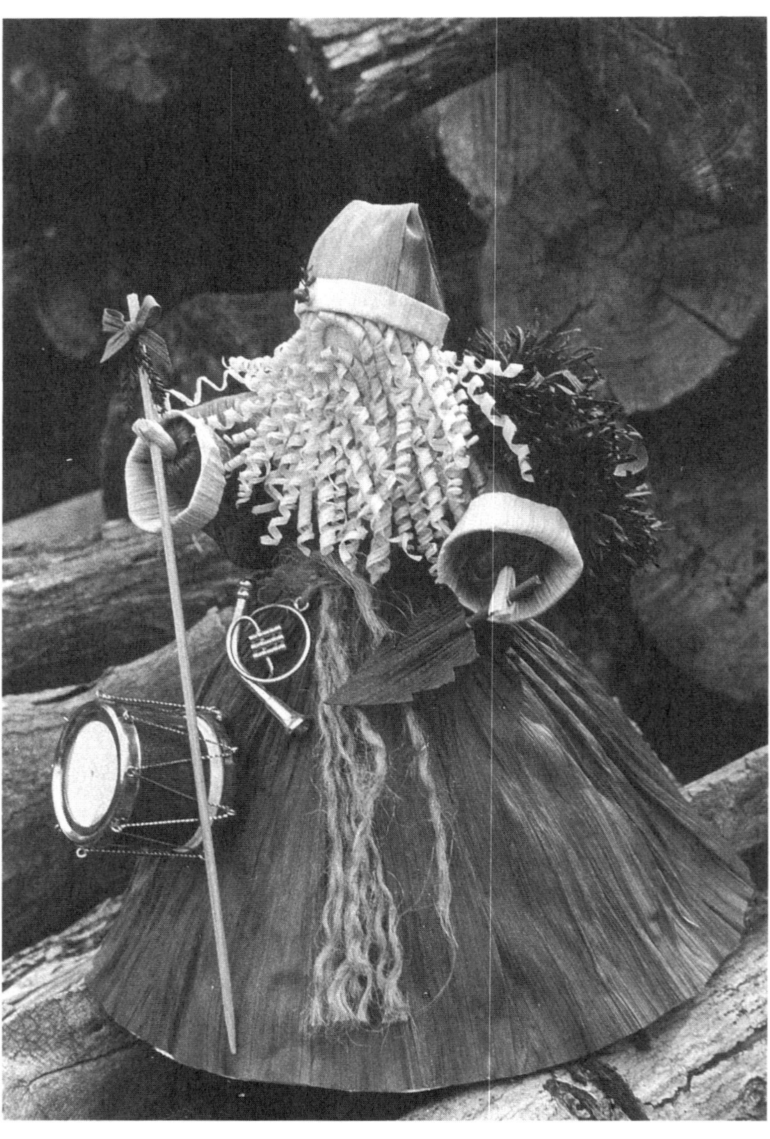

Beard of "Noel" is wound around a dowel.

doll designed after me. I used to quilt. I made the doll holding a quilting hoop. It wasn't that difficult, and I got better and better."

Next was a pioneer doll, named for her sister Theresa, who had moved to Colorado. Theresa has a bundle of wood on her back. Mary, created for her artist sister, has a palette and paintbrush. Maureen, for a sister who was a new mother, holds a baby. Janine, for a sister in college, carries schoolbooks. Rene, originated for her youngest sister, has a doll at her side.

"That's how I did it," Anne remembers. "Then I started

IOWA FOLK ARTISTS

making them for friends." She made a teacher at Christmas for her son's second-grade teacher. A bride and angel in natural cornhusks followed. "I must have always wanted to do an angel."

There were no samples or patterns to follow. She just used ingenuity and hard work, and the dolls followed. She made black dolls and miniature dolls and animals. She made a bridal set wearing copies of the dresses of a real bride and bridesmaids. An ordained minister wanted a doll with a Bible in hand. "One woman called who had adopted a Korean baby. So I made a mother with a Korean baby."

The magnificence of her art is that she can take simple, earthy cornhusks and transform them into dolls so regal that someone once bought three to take to a wedding in a French castle. "It just made me feel good to take something that is nothing and turn into something beautiful," she says humbly. "The farmers throw the husks away, and they go down into the ground."

She sold her dolls at Winterset's Covered Bridge Festival and other regional festivals. Her dolls are so carefully constructed and so beautifully created that her reputation as an artist spread. An advertising agency in Minneapolis called her. Every year the company searches out an artist to create an original angel as a Christmas gift to clients.

"One of their employees saw my doll. They wrote and asked if I'd be interested in doing eight hundred angels. I figured I'd have to do it wholesale, and I was not going to do it," she remembers. "I didn't answer the letter."

The company was persistent and wrote again. They called. They would give her two years for this project. She asked for money up front, expecting to deter them. "They sent me a check for one-third of the money and didn't know who I was. I asked them to design a box. They designed a box with a gold foil insert so it would bend over and hold the doll in place. They sent a semi-truck here and dropped the boxes."

Anne worried that there could be a fire or flood. So the company sent down a truck to pick up a load of dolls—not an easy task since she lives on a steep gravel road.

But she soon discovered two years was not enough time to make eight hundred individual dolls at a comfortable pace. "I felt like a factory. We'd watch TV, and I'd be ripping cornhusks in strips. My hands would get cramps. You have to work when

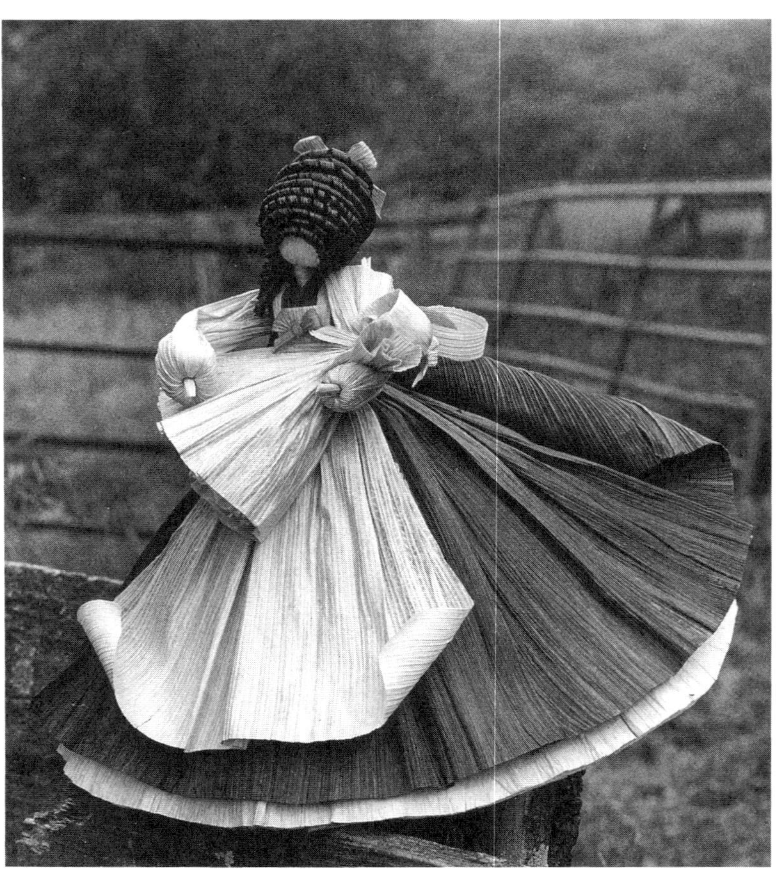

they are wet. Your hands are always wet. I'd be up until two or three in the morning all by myself working on those dolls—trying to get the last one done. I had to make one more. My husband would help me box them up."

By the time she had made her eight-hundredth doll, she was saying to herself, "Is this ever going to be over? I felt like this was a job. I was tickled. This was an honor. But that was a year I had twenty shows booked. I tried to do too much.

"It was a lonely job working in the laundry room. It was a mess. I could never get away. It got so I wanted to see someone. I felt trapped with them. I left when it became a business." In five or six years, in the late 1980s, she made over three thousand dolls.

Her dolls are pure cornhusk. All of them have billowing gowns that suggest Scarlett O'Hara more than wrappers around ears of corn. To make these, she gathers cornhusks as if gathering a skirt and secures them with wire. She continues to fill in with cornhusks until the dresses stand out like ball-

IOWA FOLK ARTISTS

gowns. For her angels she uses a cardboard cone as a form under the dress. Two layers of husks go over the base. She creates angel wings by folding over cornhusks and scalloping and cutting them. "When you wet the husks, they are really pliable." She has never counted how many cornhusks are in each doll. "It's just a feel—a whole feel."

Her dolls have formal ringlets so real that they look as if they have been rolled on a curling iron. She thinks it's the "hair more than anything" that makes her dolls special. "I have never seen the hair done like that before," she comments. Each hairdo takes about a half hour. She has to wet the husks, shred them, wind the strips on the dowel, dry and remove them, and clip the ends before securing them on the dolls. "I got as fast as someone who knits."

Although no features are drawn or painted on the faces, the heads' natural and expressive positions suggest the faces are real.

Anne has never timed herself while making a doll. Each doll, she guesses, takes several hours to make. It takes, at least,

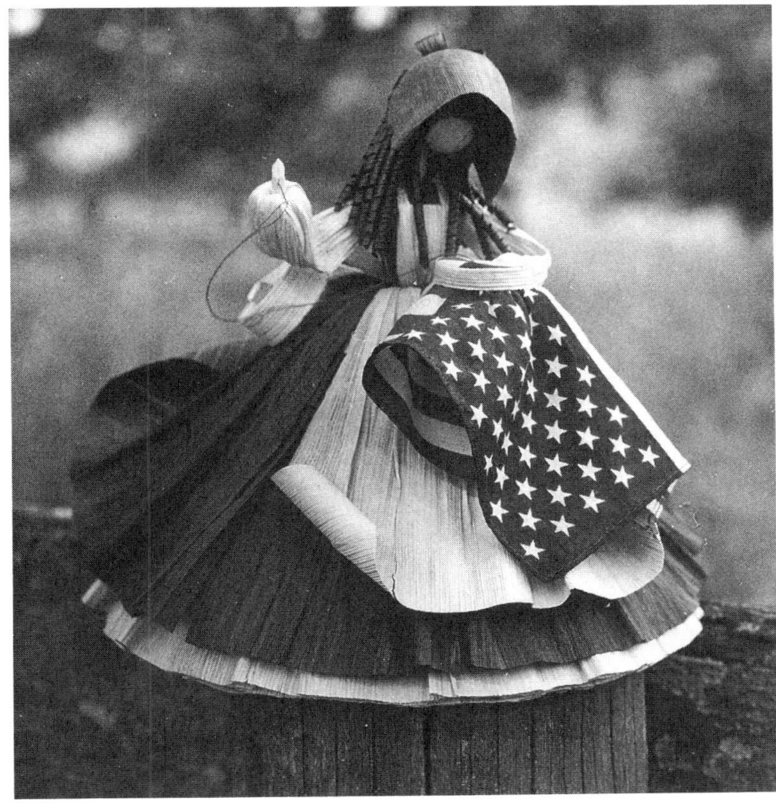

"Betsy" is an example of the glamour of Anne's cornhusk dolls.

a half hour just for the hair. What makes them beautiful? The answer comes slowly. "I don't know."

Being tied to the laundry room making so many dolls had other consequences besides loneliness. She was also eating, gaining weight. "I was closer to the refrigerator," she recalls. In 1988 she joined Weight Watchers and lost eighty-eight pounds.

This not only got her away from the solitude of the laundry room, it ultimately led to a people-oriented career. As a Weight Watchers leader she gives motivational lectures all over Des Moines. "I was overweight all my life. This is a treasure. I can help those people now. You have to go through it to help other people." She also helps her husband, who is in the auto repair business, with his books.

Anne is sophisticated and natural at the same time. She is contemporary, fast-moving, outgoing, and obviously happy. She sits on the porch of her house that overlooks a pond and woods. It is next to the farm where her parents live, the farm on which she was raised. She talks about the neighbor who made the hickory nut dolls. She is in her nineties, in a rest home. Her daughter-in-law recently gave Anne a hickory doll, which she cherishes. She gets up and goes to look for the dolls.

"I wish I knew where I came up with that hair on my dolls. It could be. ... I'm sure everything we take in from the past, we store away in our memories."

She credits Iowa's corn with being an influence on her love of cornhusk dolls. "Someone in the city who never saw corn would never think about this. If you grow up on a farm in Iowa, you'd better be familiar with corn," says Anne. "I don't know if that influenced me or not. I had to weed corn out of the beans. I had to cultivate corn, I had to pick corn, and I had to feed it to the pigs."

She likes the fact that Indians were making figures out of cornhusks before the settlers arrived. "Indians years ago made little dolls for the kids to play with out of cornhusks. That's the part I love—taking something of nature and turning it into art. I think this is one of the folk arts that's most difficult. Woodworking seems easier. I'm going through a process—creating with my hands—pulling on wire. My hands split."

Anne picks up a handful of cornhusks and pinches them together as if making a skirt. Her talent as a folk artist, a maker of cornhusk dolls, is not lost and never will be. One day she wants to return to the art, but in a different way. She is collecting ideas for new specialty dolls, such as Penny Pockets. The dolls will be detailed and limited edition. She would do a certain number and retire the doll.

"It's hard to believe I did it. I would like to make them again. All I can think of is the work. It was my own fault I let it get out of control. I couldn't say no. People would call and ask. People still call and beg me. I just haven't done it.

"I will never forget how to make them," she says.

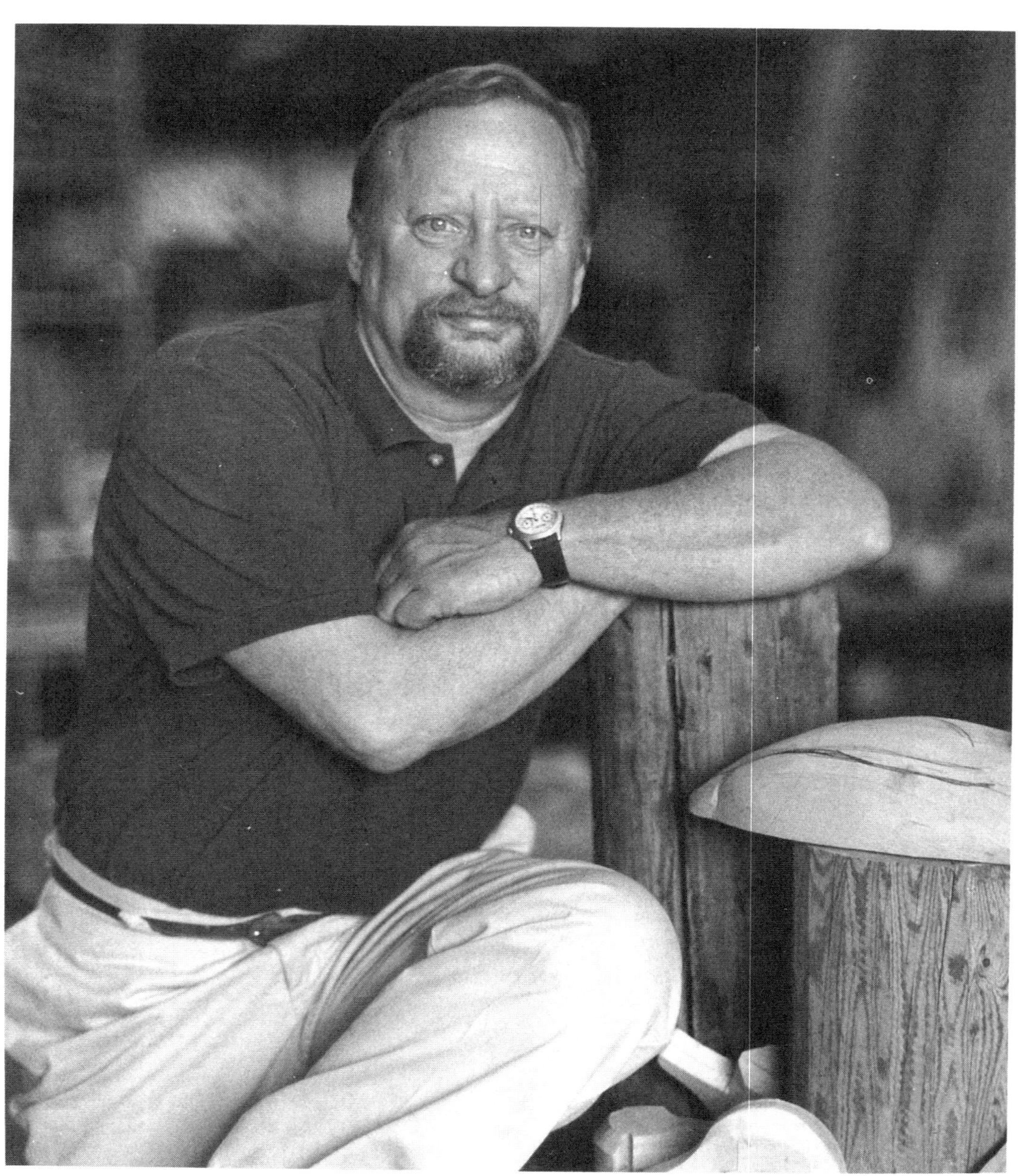

JOE LAURENZO

Joe Laurenzo: "I tried to picture old farmers making decoys in the off-season to supplement their income. I tried to picture them sitting in an unheated shed with old tools—how they would do it. I tried to picture old gunners who bought the decoys. They were a tool for them. They wanted the silhouette of the bird so they could shoot lots of birds and sell to restaurants. They were getting meat for the market. It wasn't a sport.

"I never sat and looked for perfect wood. The farmers had an old stump or something. From hunting a lot you get a look of the real bird opposed to what most people see as a duck. When I'm carving these decoys, I have these things in my mind. I use old tools. That's how I do it. I try to paint with old paints if I can find them. I base mine on old decoy patterns. They're kind of stylistic. The colors are right but not realistic."

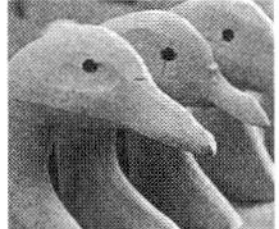As a youngster Joe Laurenzo liked to hunt, but he couldn't afford decoys, so he made them. "I did some reading," he recollects. "I made a few ugly ones out of materials at hand." As a high school freshman, he asked for a table saw for Christmas. "It was a little strange. Not many high school kids ask for that. I taught myself. My grandparents and dad believed in working. A lot of it came from necessity. I didn't have money to buy a boat, so I built one. It was a challenge."

The woodworking and decoys had to be shelved for a few years while he packed adult responsibility onto his shoulders at an early age. His father, a second-generation Italian and the owner of restaurants in Des Moines, developed serious heart trouble. Joe, being the oldest, went to work. "From the age of fifteen on, I ran the restaurant. I didn't want to. All that stuff plays into ...," his voice trails. "When you're the oldest in the family, you have to be the responsible one."

He went to work before and after school. He sometimes cooked the whole menu, washed pots and pans, and did the firing. "He didn't want confrontation so I had to do the firing. If we needed a dishwasher from the Bethel Mission, I'd go pick him up."

Double duty continued through his college years. He commuted thirty miles to Iowa State University, where he majored in engineering, and returned to run the restaurant in the evening. He finished these wearying years when he graduated with a business degree from Drake University in Des Moines.

It was after college, while selling ads for *Look* magazine, that dormant thoughts of decoys were revived. "My boss was into antique gambling equipment, so we stopped at every flea market and antique store. I got reinterested in decoys and bought a few antique ones."

He remembers that at about that time a major book came out on decoy collecting. "The prices went sky-high after that, and I couldn't buy anymore." Then one day he wandered through a woodcarvers' show in a mall and was mesmerized by what he saw. "I thought, 'I'm going to try that.' I started making decoys. That was twenty-five years ago."

In his exhausting days balancing the restaurant business

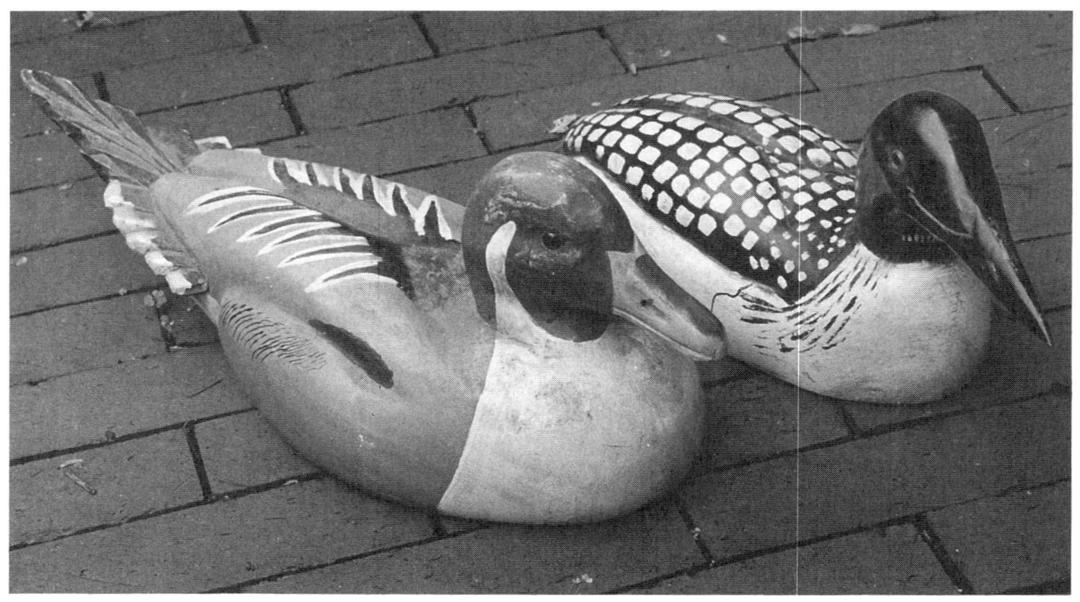

with school, he had learned, "Whatever I do, I do the best I can." To make his decoys the best, he hunted for old ones to study. "I'd talk to people at shooting and fishing memorabilia shows. I'd ask if they knew where any old decoys were or if they knew any makers or old hunters. I wanted to see if they had anything left in their sheds. There was a lot more junk than good stuff out there. At the time I didn't know that I was more and more interested. It was just evolving. I started carving, carving pretty heavy, learning."

On a hunch he took eight or ten decoys to sell at a Fourth of July show in Indianola. "I didn't sell any," he remembers. "You had to be depressed, but no one was buying anything that day." It was later, at an Isaac Walton League auction, that he sold his first decoy. "I felt great. Someone wanted a decoy bad enough to buy my stuff. That was the bug that bit me. When I figured out what the right shows were, I started selling so much, I couldn't keep up."

This natural understanding of wood and construction led, almost in an unconscious way, toward a career. After *Look* magazine folded, Joe sent out resumés. Before there were any answers, someone asked him to build a garage. "I can look at a garage and see how it would go together in these steps," Joe says. "I'm not afraid to tackle stuff. It all falls back to building furniture when I was a kid and that stuff. A lot of it came from necessity. I liked to do it."

IOWA FOLK ARTISTS

Perhaps it was because he had had an early career in the Italian food business that Joe did not go into the business of his father and grandfather. Instead, he reached two generations back to Tuscany and his great-grandfather who had been a bridge builder. "Maybe it was in the genes," Joe says in a believe-it-or-not sort of way. "There were lots of bridges in Tuscany that he built." His great-grandfather later came to America with his son, Joe's grandfather, but he couldn't learn the language and returned home.

Joe makes a living with a business specializing in restoration—cabinetry, complicated staircases, church altars. It is the sort of business that takes the same sincerity and care that Joe gives to his decoys. "It's a challenge. I love the tools. Not many people are doing it, so you get known for it and get calls. I haven't advertised since I have been in business."

Blue-eyed, blond, and distinguished with a goatee, Joe sits casually in his bright, spacious studio with piles of unfinished duck heads on a bench behind him. There is a thoughtfulness about him that is understandable. He walks to a corner and drags out a large canvas bag. This is his carving bag, he explains, as he pulls out a perfectly crafted wren and sanderling. He has always admired and liked old craftsmanship, old joinery. "If I go into a store and open a drawer, and it's not dovetailed, I'm not interested. I like fine workmanship, whether I do it or someone else."

He walks to his truck with the license plate DECOY and points to the gaggle of unfinished duck heads rolling around the back. "I pull them out and start carving," he muses. He has even carved duck heads while ice fishing. "My friend complained that the chips were falling into the ice hole." He is serious, but he smiles.

Joe's ducks, geese, and shorebirds look authentic enough that, hollowed out and sitting on water, they would be unrecognizable from live birds. "My work changed when I started studying individual birds. You have to know the wood duck, the mallard. Then you have to get the attitude—what it looks like sitting on water.

"To me each duck has a look or attitude I try to get in carving. I tried to get each individual species. You see mallards [decoys] with too big a neck and pintails [decoys] with too small a neck. People know something is wrong, but they can't put a finger on it."

JOE LAURENZO

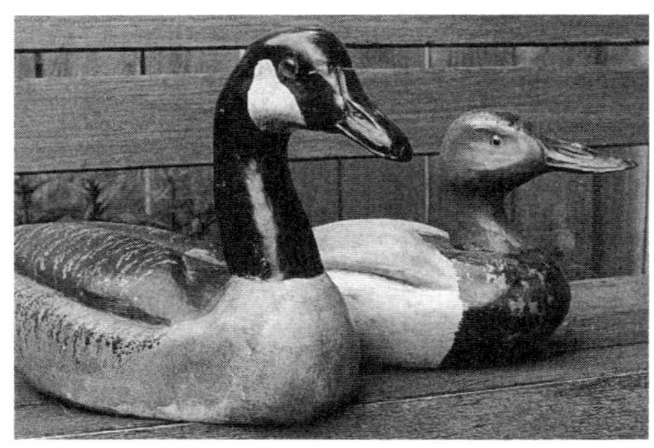

Canada goose and canvasback in Joe's studio.

His love of craftsmanship, above all, is apparent in his decoys. "Everything is handmade. I cut out one at a time. I have no reproduction-type equipment."

Important to Joe in his carving is a shaving horse that he made years ago. "I copied it from an old Swiss cooper who made wooden barrels. I saw the man making wooden barrels and thought that'd work for a decoy carver."

Joe sits on the shaving horse and, with his foot, controls the vice holding the duck's body. This leaves both hands free to hold his draw knife. The advantage is that he can lift his foot and change the positions of the duck's body. He makes his draw knives out of straight-edged razors. His favorite tool is the chisel. "It's the hand control," he says. "I like to put old tools on decoys. If they're done on the machine, you can tell they're done on the machine."

His decoys are further enhanced through his painting. He reveals that he uses regular oil base enamel, but the technique, one he developed because he wasn't a good painter, is something he won't impart. "When people come to classes, they come to find out how I get the paint on there. It's not fair to my customers to tell."

Joe studies birds constantly. "If I'm driving on the interstate, I may be watching hawks. If I know where ducks and geese are, I will stop at a reservoir." When he talks about his favorite bird to carve, the canvasback, it is obvious that he knows it as if it were the family cat. "I like that head. It has a big neck. He is regal." His sandpipers, herring and laughing gulls, and plovers perch as if ready to hop off their stands made from old telephone poles.

Recently an organization asked Joe to make one thousand ducks for its members. At first he thought, "Oh, great." Then he realized if he ever did it he'd never go back to making decoys by hand again. "I'd be hiring some people to paint white and others to paint black. ... My intent is to perpetuate the art of decoy making. I don't like phony stuff. That's why I do it this way."

Even though he has more than enough restoration business, Joe never gets too far from his decoys. Not far from his house, he has a spacious warehouse shop where he carves. "If I haven't done anything for a month, I have to get away for a night and carve. Often I'm supposed to be doing something else, and I'll sneak out and carve. It's such good relaxation. It's good for the mind. You get a clear head."

He seems as if he's always relaxed although there are hints of restlessness when he talks about sleep. "I don't like to go to bed until I'm too tired to stay awake. I can't watch TV or movies. There are too many things to do. I love to get up in the morning. I love what the day brings."

There is no doubt that his grandfather, who was born in Italy, symbolized for Joe the idea that working hard is how to lead your life. "He was uneducated formally. He was absolutely brilliant. He sat and read encyclopedias. He worked. How he worked. He worked seven days a week until the work was done. He worked until the day he died."

It's not unusual for Joe to be working on business projects in the early hours of the morning in order to do everything he needs to do. "I may do decoys at ten in the morning, then business at one in the morning. I'm my own boss, so I do what I do," he says.

Joe's pretty blond wife, Linda, shares his love of birds and enjoys going to shows with him. Their children, Brian, Jill, and Eric, are grown. Linda works full time as finance officer for the Iowa State Senate. Summer evenings they enjoy walking together through their Des Moines neighborhood.

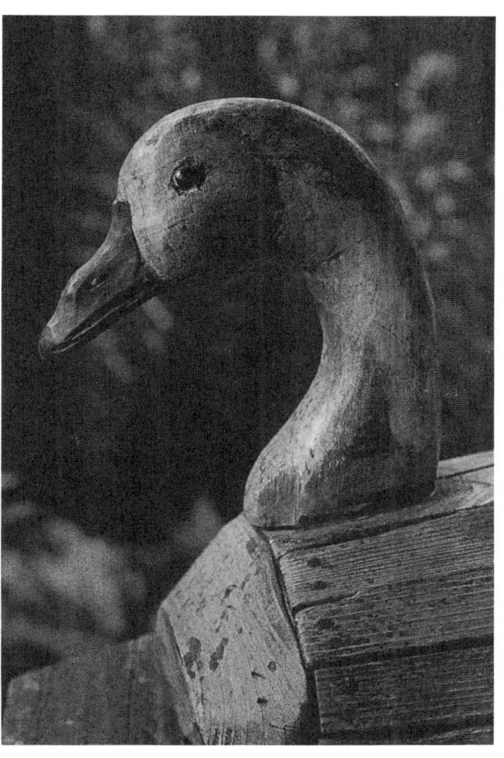

Slat snow goose depicts Joe's talent.

Joe believes that he must hand down his art, so he teaches some adult education classes. "Some of the old retired guys— it's amazing what it does for them. They can pick up and put down. It's clean. Tools last forever. I'm amazed at people who get hooked."

As for hunting: "I still hunt. I'm not the killer that I was. It's more important to be out with the dog and watching." He looks away. "I'm not opposed to hunting though."

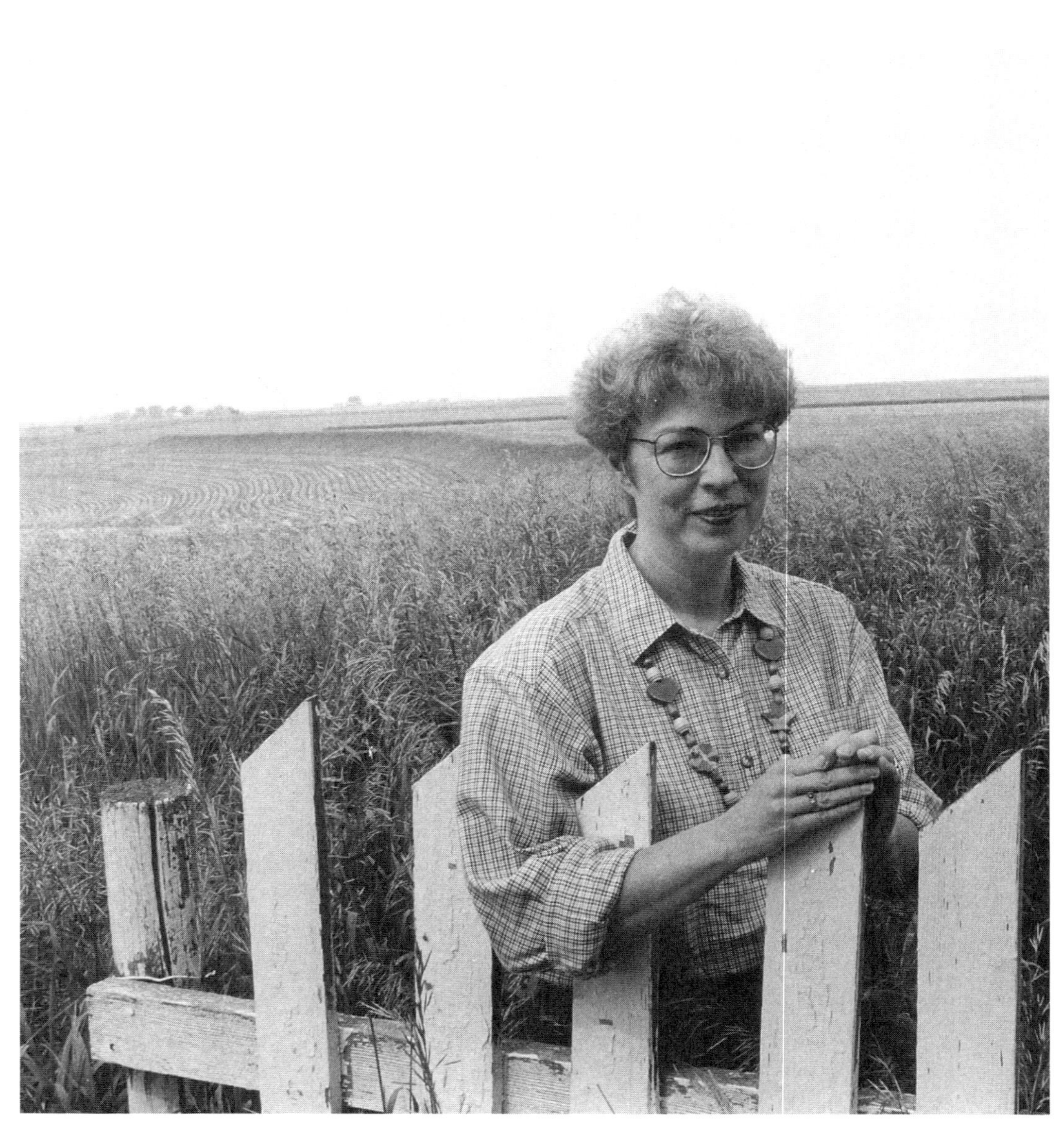

DONNA WOOD

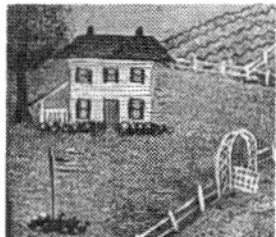

In the mid-1970s when American farming hit hard times, Donna Wood, a city girl transplanted to a western Iowa small town, started painting farm scenes on saws to pay some household expenses. News of her talent spread by word of mouth across the western counties. "People brought me old family saws and pictures of their farms. They'd say, 'Here's our barn. Here's our house.' I didn't have a sense of how they related to each other, so I'd drive to the farms and sketch them so I'd know where the crib was—where the barn was."

Folks brought her long saws, handsaws, and skill saws. "I'd clean up the saw, soak the brass screws in lemon juice and salt. I'd take the handle off and scrub the saw down. I'd use Rustoline paint to seal it down." She charged from $5 to $35 per saw. "I didn't count labor. I was going to be home anyway. There were tough times on the farm in those years."

In five years she painted over a thousand saws. Clients wanting their farmsteads commemorated on saws were usually men. Today she paints primitive, innocent farm scenes on wood. Remembering the saws, she says, "That was training. I got landscape-type training. I can see it in the primitives—the way I do the background and the foreground."

Donna, tall, with a natural, healthy beauty and a quiet sense of herself, has an unaffected give-and-take relationship with the components of farm life. She records this life in her paintings as if to ensure the scenes don't drift away.

She walks to a window of the big yellow house on the hill, often the house in her paintings. She looks across the vista toward Walnut, a well-preserved rural town with a brick main street stretching from cornfield to cornfield. "I hate it when the corn is high, and my view is blocked," she laments. "In the fall I can look and tell when the ball game is on because the lights are on at the ballpark."

In the shady backyard, with an I've-got-a-secret attitude, she lifts a wooden lid from above a basement window. Cuddled on the landing is a litter of kittens. Four kittens from another litter prance across the yard toward her. She picks up a kitten and strokes it as if it were the only one. At that moment

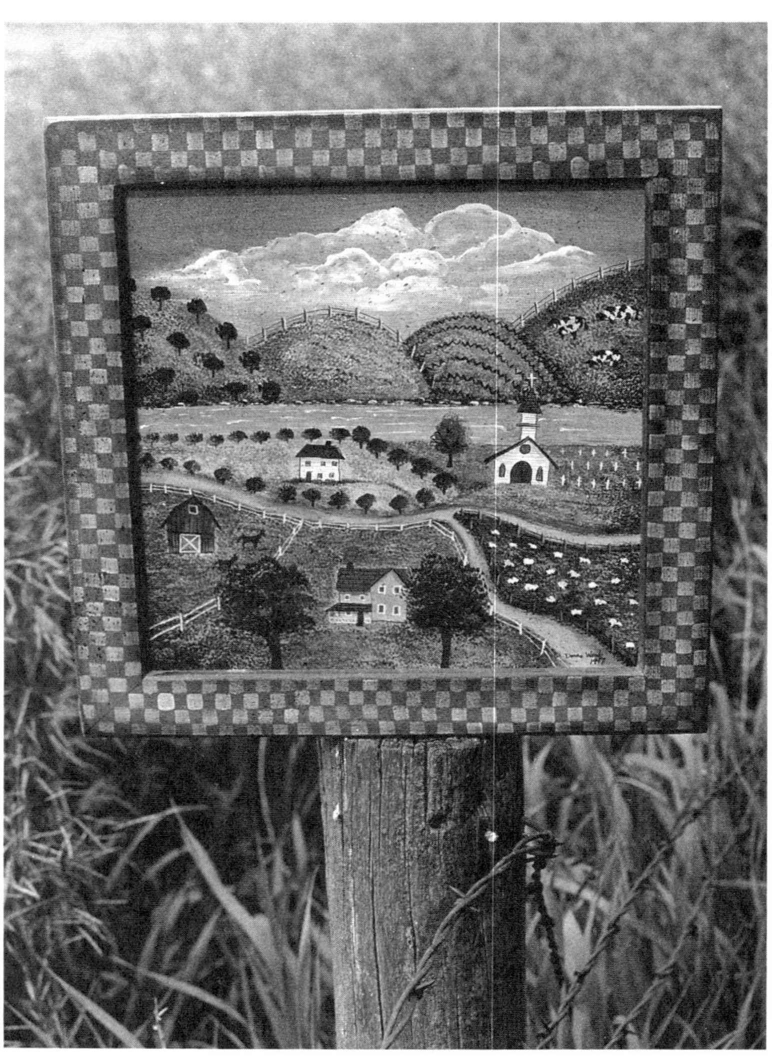

she admits to having eighteen cats. "I feed and kiss every one everyday," she claims.

Not surprisingly, she rarely paints a primitive without a cat in the scene. She captures with her paintbrush on wood the particulars of Iowa—the barns, houses, children, corn, cows, sheep, and chickens. With the familiarity of someone born on a farm, she portrays rural Iowa as a beautiful and happy land.

She cannot explain how her paintings—always cheerful with rolling hills and blue sky—evolve. She says simply that they come from within. "Sometimes I have a vision of what I want to do. I could add this or that. I don't know if I can explain it."

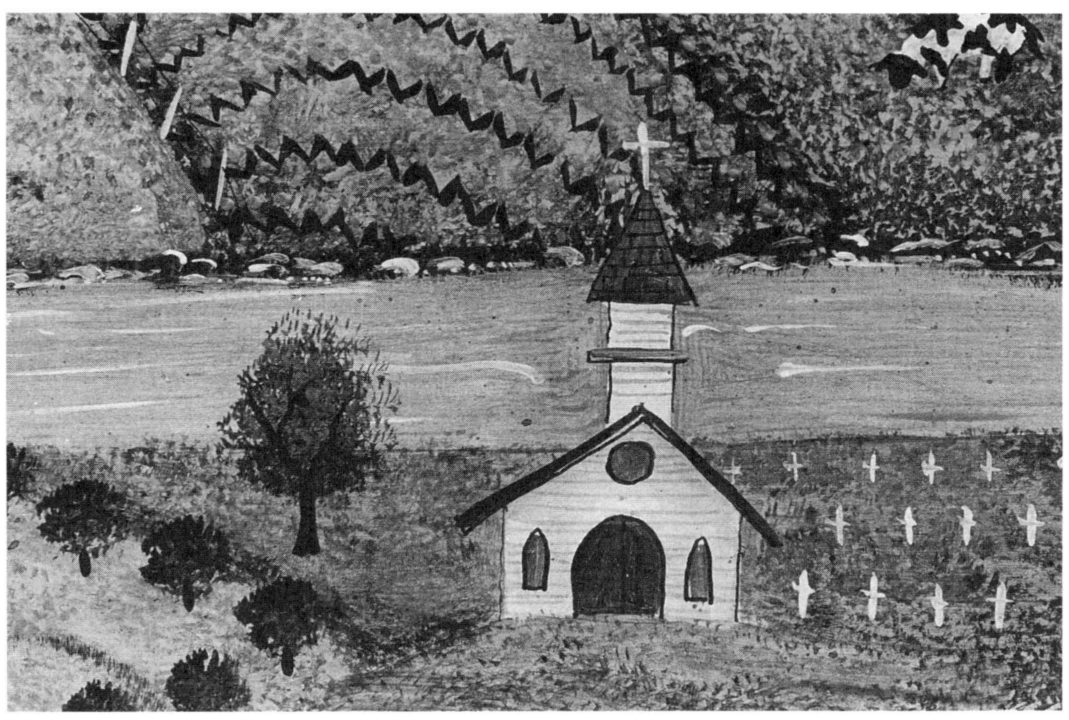

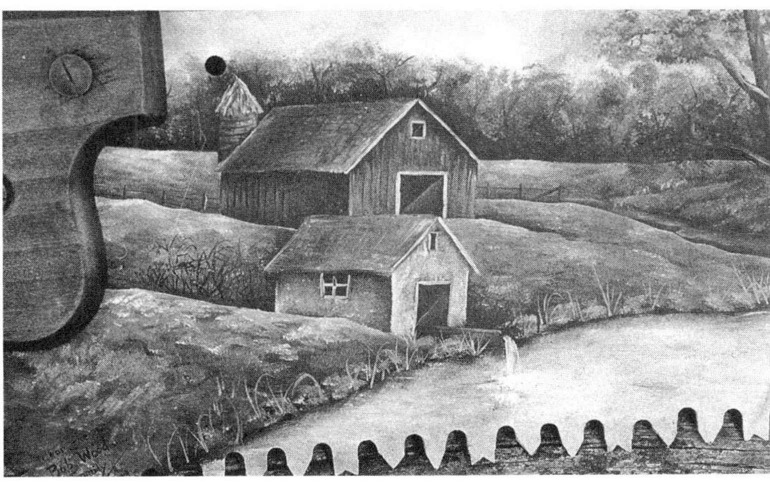

Close-up shows detail of a Donna Wood primitive.

Donna painted farm scenes on saws such as this for years.

She paints the fields first—cornfields and pastures that she sees everyday. "Then I stick things in those areas. This might be when I put in a house. This might be when I put in a barn."

She looks at a primitive with a graveyard. "I've never put a graveyard in a primitive before. I don't know where it came from. I guess it went with the church." She can explain the sheep because she sees sheep every day. There's an American flag. "I needed something else in there." The gate. "That's the gardening influence." She pauses. "Sometimes I don't know how I do something."

In her old-fashioned and often wet basement, she paints with acrylics and cuts wood with a small scroll saw. She decorates frames for all of her primitives and incorporates them into the work. "I don't like plain frames. When I do a primitive, I think, 'what can I do to enhance the painting colorwise?'"

It is obvious that Donna savors all aspects of her rural environment. In reality she calls herself a city girl from Streeter and Dwight, Illinois, actually not big towns in a state that claims Chicago. She met her husband, Bob, who was born in Atlantic, Iowa, when he was selling grain dryers in Illinois and she was a college student with a summer waitressing job. "When I met him, I knew he loved the farm. I thought that

*Donna's frames
complete her primitives.*

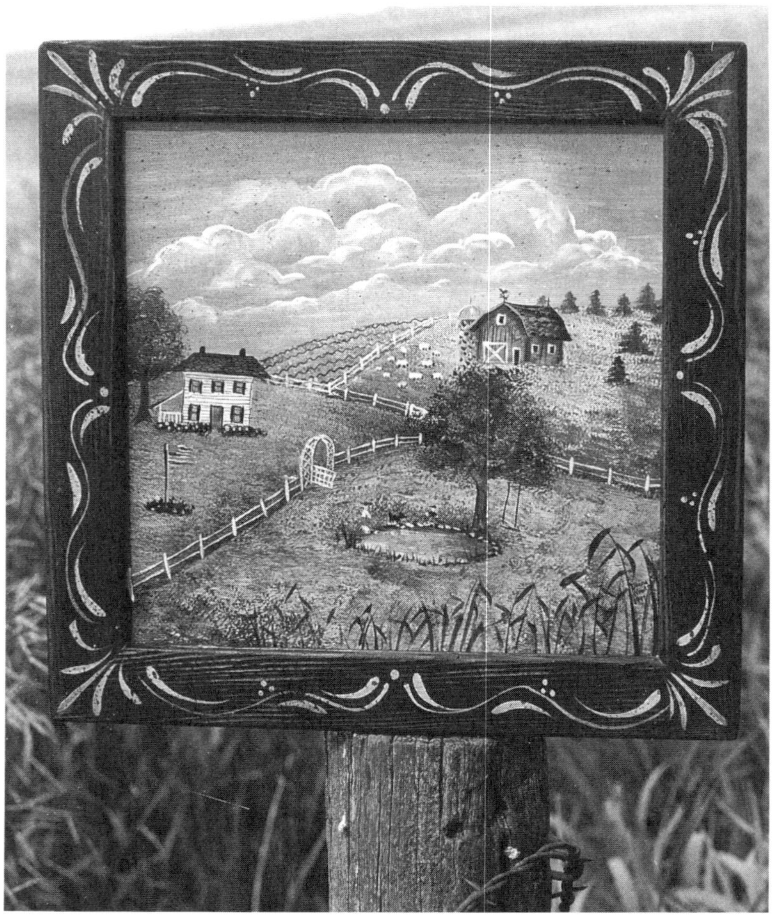

IOWA FOLK ARTISTS

was in the distant future. We'll cross that bridge when we come to it. I knew that was Bob's dream."

Not long after they were married, one of Bob's friends called to tell him about a farm for sale near Walnut, which is up the road from Atlantic. She still remembers when he brought her to see the farm. "As I turned the corner of the gravel road, I felt I was coming home. Now that I've been here, I love it. I thought I was a city person until I got here." Without hesitation she planted a huge garden, canned vegetables, froze sweet corn.

At some point she also painted a primitive that she put in a Farm Bureau show and sold for $20. "I labored in the basement. I couldn't wait to show Bob and get his feedback. 'I hope you don't waste time on those,' he said. Why do I care what he likes? I was crushed. I've learned to trust my instincts. If he likes something, I don't. If I like it, he doesn't. He's a reverse barometer. I paint to please myself.

"He's a down-to-earth, plans-for-the-future manager. I'm in la la land, planning something in my head. We're exact opposites."

While Donna's scenes on saws helped during the days of a down farm economy, her primitives helped later. At one point she and Bob heard about an old parish house that was for sale for $500. They planned to fix it up and sell it at a profit. "We had to buy acreage," she remembers. "We had to put in plumbing and fix the foundation. We had thousands in it. We went months without selling it. We were at the bottom of our resources and didn't know if we would have to ask my parents for help.

"We had enough to survive—nothing extra. One year I killed myself painting, but it helped us get over a bad time. I was painting until three or four in the morning every day and getting up and starting over. You do what you have to do at the time."

Donna remembers this painting as giving her enjoyment and, beyond that, self-satisfaction. "Feminism was just coming in. People would say, 'Oh, what do you do?' I'd say, 'I'm on a hog farm and raising a family.' I could see on their faces that wasn't good enough. I was happy. Painting gave me an outlet to be accepted by others. I was glad I could stay home with children and still help support the family."

It is difficult to separate Donna's primitives from her long and deep fondness for quilts, another rural art. Her primitives often feature a clothesline with a quilt hanging on it, and there's a quilt-like detail to her paintings. Quilts were very much a part of her painting in the transition from painting scenes on saws to the primitives. For awhile she cut quilt block designs out of wood and painted them with great detail right down to the stitches. She strung these into necklaces.

This love of quilts and quilting is a gift from her grandmother who used to make quilts in the depression. "She had a young family, huge garden, oil lamps. She worked out of old scraps. She took cotton from natural cotton. That was her batting—with the cotton seeds in it." Donna remembers talking to her grandmother about quilting. "Something in me must have been in her too."

One time her grandmother sent a bundle of old quilt blocks to Donna, a gift Donna will never forget. "My mom was one of ten kids, and I got grandma's quilt blocks. I put one group into a quilt. Others I haven't done. I feel privileged my grandma wanted me to have those."

Donna herself has made forty to fifty quilts in about fifteen years. They feature the same happy colors as her primitives. "I remember thinking that if I could do a quilt in a lifetime wouldn't that be great. I have twelve started, and twenty in my head. Twelve are started because I have these visions in my head. I start something to see what it might be like and have to go off and start something else." She holds up a bright lone star quilt pieced with vivid fabrics in novel colors. It has an unusual and complicated border. "I don't know how I did the border," she says.

The desire to be different started early. In first grade everyone was to name his or her favorite color. "It was blue, blue, blue. I took orange because no one else wanted it. I don't want to fit in."

Perhaps this need to be different helped Donna to overcome major discouragement from a teacher. "My seventh-grade teacher said, 'You don't have talent.' I wanted to do things but thought I couldn't because I didn't have talent." She excelled in math. "Everyone thought I'd be a brain. They never saw the other side of me. I look back, and I was always creative. I never thought of myself as that growing up."

For a long time she didn't have confidence in her work and would try to imitate the work of other artists. "Now I have the drive within myself to try my own things. I trust my own instincts now."

In fact, her daughter Sarah has been working at a gift shop, and people ask who her parents are. "Bob is known as an outgoing guy who always has a story to tell—a salesman's personality. I'm known by my work," Donna admits modestly.

The Woods have added to their original eighty acres; now they have 355. "In five years we'll have all the farms paid off and can take vacations and do the other things we haven't done before."

She looks at the carpet in the living room. "We've had to be careful. This carpeting has been down fifteen years. Last three or four years we should have gotten a new carpet—but with two girls in college. ... We've always had secondhand cars, but we've never felt deprived."

She has loved the farm and the small town as places to raise children Sarah, Becky, and Aaron, who are now grown. "When we moved here, I wasn't sure what I wanted to do, but it was a great way to raise children because I believe in teaching the work ethic. We've had such wonderful memories of family—working and playing together. And, we've had lots of time to be together as a family.

"Becky used to tell me she hated it when I yelled upstairs, 'We've got chores to do.' Now they've seen it pay off as they've had to work for others and had responsibility. They've known how to work, and others haven't. We've always been happy."

Donna admits that she could be at peace at home on the farm alone. "I love winter when I'm stuck in the house and do all these things. I can always find things I want to do. I hope I live long enough. There's joy in work. To have work and have something turn out well is one of the greatest satisfactions there is."

From above a door in the living room, Donna lifts a saw with a scene. "I still get calls about saws, and I haven't done any for ten years."

But she's already thinking about the wedding gifts she plans to make for her daughters. "I want to paint our farm with hogs in the hog lot and the three dogs we've had and the raspberry patch. ..."

DONNA WOOD

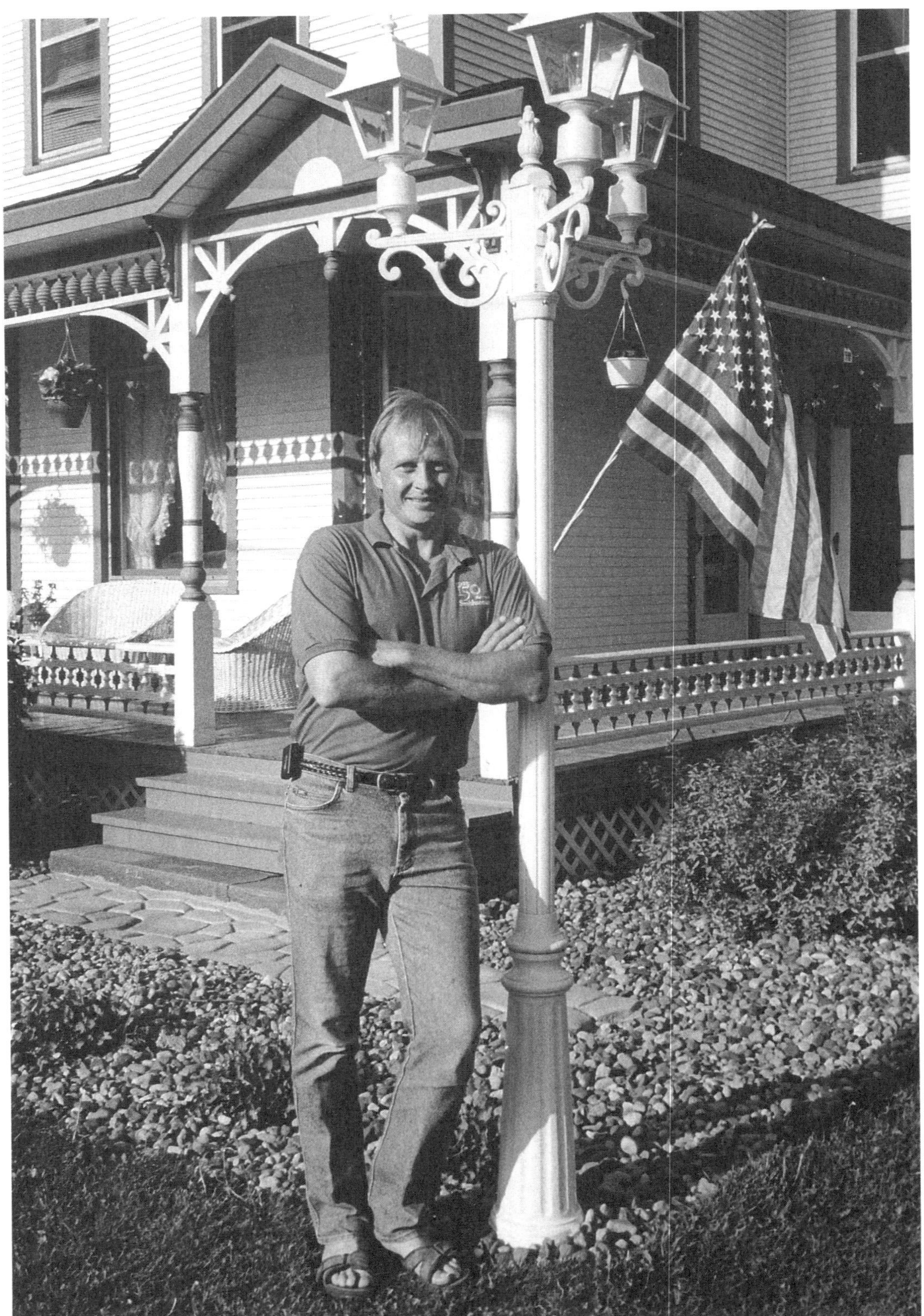

RODNEY SEITZ

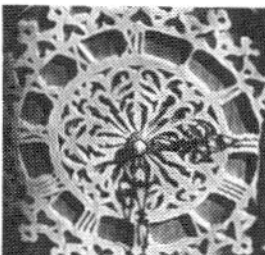

It all started one day in 1979 when Lyle Olson, a Clermont clockmaker, saw a large oak log lying in Rodney Seitz's yard. He wanted the wood to make clocks and offered to trade Rodney one of his fretwork clocks for the log. The trade was made, and Lyle started making a Creation Clock while Rodney stood and watched.

"The more I looked at the clock and studied it, the more interested I became in it," Rodney remembers. He watched while the piece of log was sawed down into the thirty delicate pieces that make a Creation Clock. Father Time was in the center, with sand and an hourglass denoting the moments in life. On the sides the clock featured guardian angels, and on top, deliverance angels. A harp in the center of the peak of the clock denoted the glory of heaven. As his part in the trade, Lyle gave the clock, similar to fretwork clocks made in late nineteenth-century workshops, to Rodney.

"I stared at it so long that I decided I wanted to try it," Rodney remembers. But there was a two-year detour while Rodney, who had dropped out of high school ("If my hands were on something, I was happier."), wandered around the country trying to get his bearings.

During this, the low point in his life, he carried the image of Lyle Olson making the Creation Clock. On return visits to Clermont he always called on Lyle. Eventually he carried the Creation Clock with him "along with a cowboy hat and a couple of pairs of jeans" as he wandered around the country. He credits Lyle and the clock as being a force that brought him back to northeast Iowa, hard work, and, ultimately, clockmaking. "I started focusing on the past and what I learned as a kid that I had never applied before. I woke up and started touching base with my roots."

When he returned to Clermont to live, he went to see Lyle, whose house was full of clocks and whose shop was in the basement. "Lyle was willing to teach me and to help me with patterns," says Rodney. "His children weren't interested in carrying on the art, so he gave me patterns and tips and sent me on my way. I always just sat and watched. I didn't ask questions. He taught me to be patient—that clockmaking wasn't something to rush into and to rush with as you're working with it. Different woods have different characteristics. He told me to treat every wood a little differently."

Rodney's hands, etched with the lines of hard work, seem too large to do fretwork, the lacy, intricate cutwork. He began by cutting twenty pieces that would be glued together to create a wildlife clock. "It was trial and error at first. The face of the clock had two deer on it. There were rabbits on the gables and bottom. The clock was filled in with oak leaves and acorns." He worked on it for five or six months.

Rodney, an electrician by trade, has the strong build of someone who by the age of ten was "hiring out"—pitching manure and haying. His straight blond hair and blue eyes project an innocence. It is easy for him to explain how he, his pretty blond wife, Brenda, and their four children recently bought a Victorian house on Spillville's Main Street, across from the Bily Clocks Museum. This is an old-fashioned Czech town where everyone knows which doors to knock on to buy just-out-of-the-oven *kolaches*, and it's Iowa's clock town.

The Bily Clocks Museum houses the intricate clocks the Bily brothers, northeast Iowa farmers, carved at the beginning of the twentieth century during the long Iowa winters. The clocks attract visitors from all over the world. The clockmaking lineage from Lyle Olson to the Bily brothers, folk heroes when Rodney was growing up, is fairly direct.

Close-up shows complexity of fretwork.

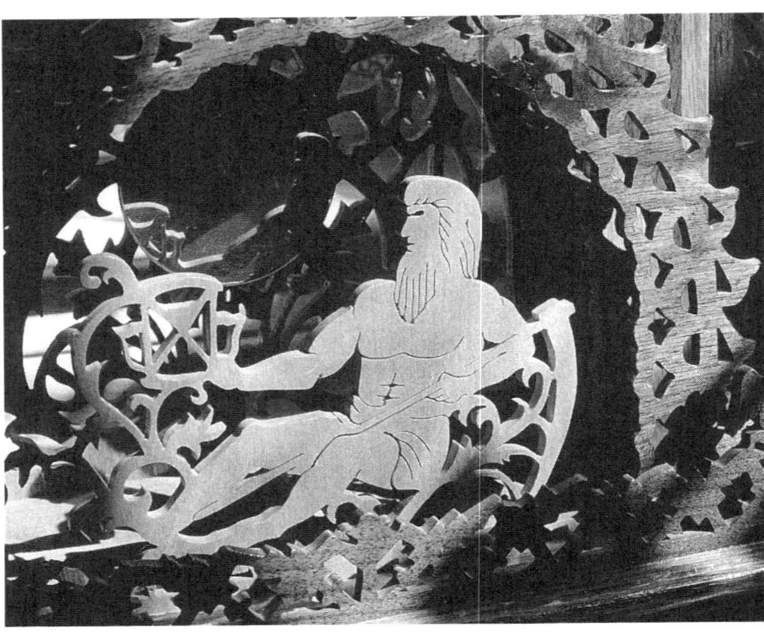

IOWA FOLK ARTISTS

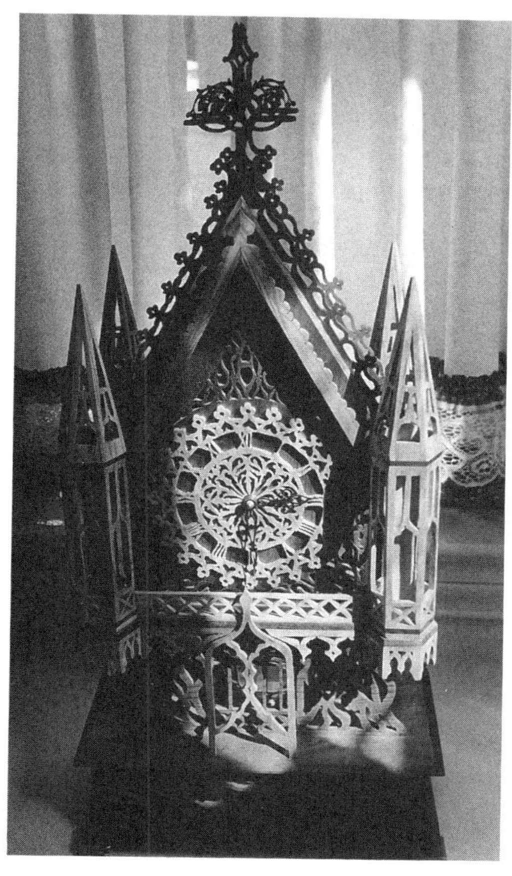

Cathedral Clock by Rodney.

Lyle had learned clockmaking from his father, Joseph, a Postville farmer and good friend of the Bily brothers. Lyle's brother, Cliff Olson of Postville, remembers stopping with his dad at the Bilys' home on rainy days before school. "They'd exchange ideas. He got patterns from them. He wanted something to do on the farm in the 1930s."

"It's a family craft," says Rodney. "If there is a problem, you get on the phone and talk to someone else who may have had a problem."

Rodney stands at the large drafting table in front of a window in the small room on the second floor of his house. He picks up a tiny picture of an eight-foot grand Gothic Altar Clock with thirty-two spires. The cathedral depicts the full life of Christ—birth, life, the twelve disciples, and the crucifixion. He found the picture in *Wild's Company Fretwork Design*, a catalogue from the 1800s. He has blown up the blurred image with a magnifying glass, but it is still small, vague, and incomplete. At the drafting table he is recreating the Gothic Altar Clock's lost design onto the tracing paper, section by section. He will work on the design three more years before he starts cutting it out of wood. "No one knows if this clock is in existence," he explains with a certain pride.

His simple, uncluttered woodworking studio, reminiscent of one from the last century, is in the garage behind the house. He sits at a foot-powered scrolling saw, which dates back to about 1865 and was manufactured by W.F. Barns Company. He found this saw, the kind that was used for creating detail in Victorian homes, at an auction in Gunder, Iowa. He also has a hand frame saw, a saw that is simply operated by hand. A bruel horse, a clamping device operated by foot and used to hold wood when using the hand frame, dates from the late 1700s.

There is an electric scroll saw also, but he tends to use the old ones. "I like to focus on the old. It's more peaceful."

The woods Rodney uses in his clocks are native to northeast Iowa—red oak, white oak, ash, walnut, honey locust, and cedar. He cuts the tree and hauls it into town, where a neighbor cuts it into five-sixteenth-inch boards. He then sands the boards to three-sixteenth inch, which is the working thickness he uses for his fretwork.

Before he cuts the wood with a scrolling saw, he makes a blueprint of a design and transfers it to the wood. After the pieces are cut, he glues, assembles, and clamps them. The Iowa Clock, one he designed for Iowa's sesquicentennial has eighty-six pieces, without the movements. The movements are Hermle, from Germany. He describes the clock. "It has an oval-shaped base with thirteen soldiers carrying flags symbolizing the thirteen original colonies. The clock is shaped like the Liberty Bell. The dial is the seal of Iowa with eagle and olive leaves. There are liberty bells placed on the clock. The state bird—the goldfinch—is in an upper corner."

For his clocks he uses a natural finish so that the beauty of the wood will show. He uses a sealer and six coats of lacquer. It takes from two months to a year to cut out and assemble a clock. "Just to create something like this out of a tree—to draw the picture and to have the finished product is real satisfying," he says.

To keep the stages of the clockmaking process going forward and to ward off tiredness, Rodney alternates between drawing patterns in his upstairs studio and either cutting or

IOWA FOLK ARTISTS

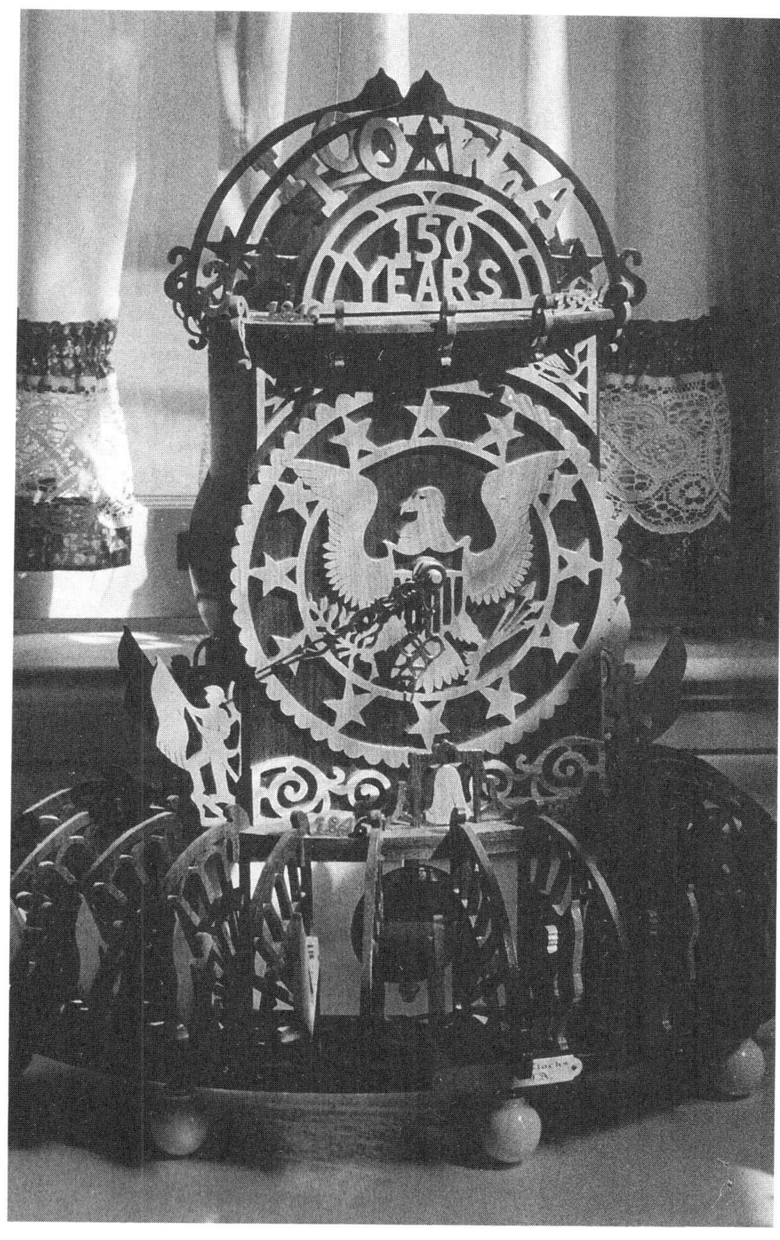

*Iowa Clock designed
and made by Rodney
for the state's
sesquicentennial.*

assembling them in the garage. He is never alone while in the garage, even in the middle of the night. "Neighbors come to the shop and talk all night long." Often his father-in-law, Allen Monroe of Decorah, helps cut and assemble. He has a nervousness about work and no time for sleep. "I lay down, and so much is going through my head that I can't sleep. If I'm going to sell a pattern, I have to be sure it's easily assembled. I think about that all night long."

RODNEY SEITZ

"Old-timers" at shows and demonstrations give Rodney some information about old designs. He also gets designs from old Wild's catalogues, which are so scarce that he often drives to a Wisconsin clockmaker's home to study a mail-order pattern book that was published in the early 1800s. Seitz, with the help of Brenda, now reproduces patterns and sends them as far away as Kuwait.

There are differences between the clocks the Bily brothers made and those made by Rodney. The Bily brothers, whose parents were born in Czechoslovakia, learned the art on their own, according to Kathleen Klimesh, manager of the Bily Clocks Museum. The Bilys hand-carved all of their clocks, whereas Rodney uses saws and makes what she calls Gothic-style clocks. Also, the Bilys threw away all of their patterns and blueprints.

Fretwork on the order of Rodney's had beginnings in Sorrento, Italy. "Travelers took the clocks from there to Scandinavia, Germany, and America," says Rodney. "The art hasn't changed a whole lot over the years. The techniques and style are the same. The means of cutting the pieces are different—instead of machines worked by hands and feet, they are electric."

Rodney demonstrated his art in 1996 at the Thirtieth Anniversary Festival of American Folk Life at the Smithsonian Institution Center for Folk Life, Progress, and Cultural Studies, in Washington, D.C.

The next skill for Rodney is learning carving. He's experimenting by doing relief carving on fretwork. He started with a wildlife clock that he redrew to make his own pattern. It has thirty pieces. "I've got full-bodied deer walking off the face of it. Below the deer are two wood ducks swimming in a stream. On the base of the clock are pheasants flying in a cluster. There are evergreen trees set back in three dimensions and ducks flying on the peak of the roof."

That Rodney should take to this folk art so effortlessly is perhaps not surprising. His aptitude for carpentry was solidifying the years he was growing up on a two-hundred-acre farm near Clermont. In his family it was part of everyday living to know how things worked so they could be repaired. "We never took anything to town. We did our own plumbing, our own bodywork, our own engine work. We did it all. We didn't have running water until I was six or seven. By then everyone else had milking machines; we didn't."

His father, a carpenter, supplemented the family income by working on cars. "For seven or eight years we would climb underneath cars and pull the motors out with an old oak tree instead of a hoist," Rodney recalls. "There was a pulley cable in the oak. We'd take the motor out and put in a new motor."

He watched his grandfather, also a carpenter, build toys and games for children. "When my grandfather died, he was building rocking horses for each of his children's families. He had just finished the last one and was at work at his bench when he died."

While he was learning how things worked, his Norwegian grandmother, Julia Molokken, was teaching him to draw. "If she was not knitting or crocheting or baking, she was drawing. She'd sit with me in the parlor or outside. She'd sit on a chair and hold a pad in her lap with pencil and paper. She always drew squirrels and bunnies."

Julia Molokken also gave her grandson an appreciation of his heritage. "I always had a fascination with old things," he says. "I would sit with my grandmother and talk about horse-drawn equipment, the way of life. My grandmother talked about getting up at dawn and cutting trees to clear the land. She'd make meals for the men. While they ate, she'd go out and drive the teams. They would work by moonlight."

One time Lyle Olson gave Rodney a ragged piece of parchment with a pattern for a Lord's Prayer Clock. "I ended up sitting down and redrawing it and piecing it back together again," Rodney remembers. He carved the clock. "It's all black walnut. The whole center is the Lord's Prayer in Norwegian. There are two pillars on each side that hold up a sunburst-type design. On the lower corners on each side, Jesus is praying. 'Amen' is underneath both silhouettes of Jesus. Outside the whole perimeter is oak leaves."

Rodney gave the clock to the Vesterheim Museum in honor of his grandmother.

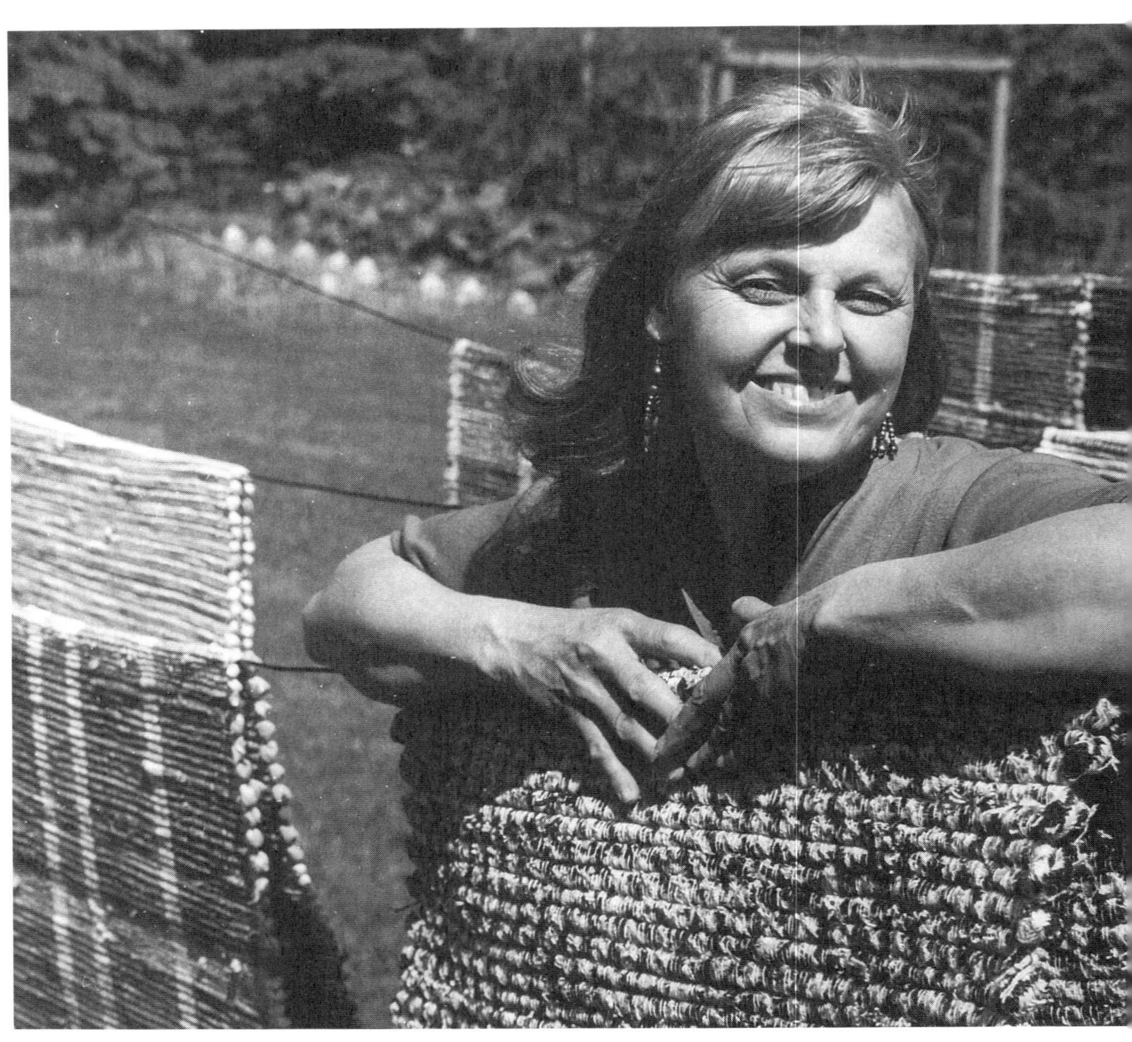

JUDY SHUROS

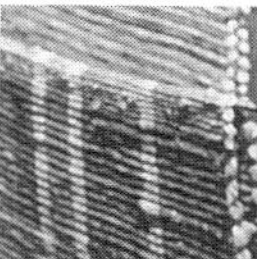 Among the wedding gifts Judy Shuros received almost thirty years ago were simple, utilitarian, old-fashioned rag rugs. A relative had woven them from "carpet rags," and Judy put them down at the front and back doors of her farmhouse, where they collected mud, snow, and dirt from boots for years.

As sometimes happens, about the time the rugs were wearing out, Judy took weaving lessons and then found an antique rug loom. "When I got my loom, the same relative and her husband came and showed me how to warp it," Judy remembers.

She has been weaving rag rugs since then. As she unwinds the rolls of carpet rags, she is connecting to strands that tie her to her grandmother. "Nineteen hundred is the part I remember. She had a garden, chickens, sheep."

Judy is a contemporary farmwife, an equal partner with her husband, Charles, in running their hog and sheep farm on the Minnesota border in northeast Iowa. Judy also raises Angora goats. On a late spring morning Judy can be found driving the tractor while she plants corn. In the afternoon she can be found in her weaving studio creating distinctive rag rugs at her almost room-sized rug loom. This is her link to a familiar bygone era that she holds close like a diary. "I'm hanging onto life of 1900 as much as I can," she says. "Country homes usually had rag rugs back years ago. I like things from the past—quilts and needlework." She remembers with fondness three rag rugs in a special room in the house in which she was raised.

Judy feels that she was a part of the earlier times that she cherishes. She grew up on a farm near Waukon and walked a quarter of a mile to the last one-room schoolhouse to be closed in Allamakee County. "There were eight grades with three or four per grade and one teacher. The older children took care of the younger ones. Lots of times the teacher was reading to the little ones, and we'd be doing history, but we'd listen anyway. That's the way it was."

Judy has an easy smile as she thinks back. "I was in that era. Going to the Living History Farms, I relive how it was. I think about how it was. It's an era that is leaving—the way our

Judy Shuros: "Harmony of color to me is very important in any kind of artwork—the influence of one color next to another color, the intensity of a color, contrast or light and darkness of a color. All of this I must consider when putting my colored rags together to weave a rug. I intend to make rugs that look balanced and pleasing to the eye."

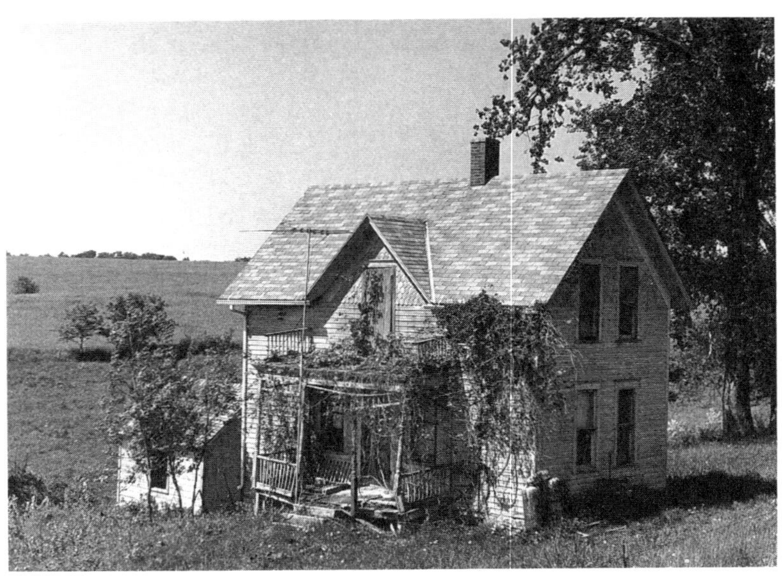

Turn-of-the-century Norwegian settlers' home, which sits on Judy's farm, will be reconstructed at a museum in Norway.

grandmother lived. The whole family had to pitch in. They were more together because they all had to help. Now they go to town and work."

The farm where Judy lives has the unchanged quiet and tranquility of earlier times. It was settled by Norwegians, and the land has a roll reminiscent of Norway. The large frame farmhouse has vistas toward a trout stream and, beyond, a verdant valley. It is silent except for the baaing of sheep and chatter of chimney swifts overhead. "I like the country," says Judy. "I like the trees, not listening to traffic, the peace and quiet."

In her weaving studio, beyond the kitchen and the sewing room, Judy, naturally pretty with blond hair and a healthy and untarnished complexion, is comfortably wearing blue jeans and a red T-shirt. At the old wooden loom in the middle of the studio, she stands and pushes the heavy beater. She is almost hidden by bushel baskets piled high with large balls of fabric in myriad colors. "I can't weave and work in the barn. Rug weaving is hard work," she explains. "I have to stand, and the beater is heavy. In a couple of hours I am tired."

She has already spent two days cutting, tearing, and sewing fabric into strips that she has wound into the balls ready for weaving. She acknowledges that she "tears when she can" but that not all fabrics tear, so she sometimes has to cut and sew. "I do up what I have and put colors together when I weave."

IOWA FOLK ARTISTS

Her rugs—usually plaid—have a uniqueness through color and texture that makes each a work of art. She cannot explain what she does. "I just do it. I start weaving and put colors together. I take the ball of fabric I have and match it with another. Sometimes I make a rug I don't like, and someone else will. I'm interested in how the colors look together. Putting different colors together makes each rug different. Rag rug weaving is fun because you always have different fabrics all the time, and each is different when it comes off the loom."

Finding old cotton fabric to use in the rugs is a never-ending search, but one she enjoys. "I like making use of old clothing and sheets," she says. Her children give her their old clothes. She frequents resale shops in search of old cotton clothing and sheets, which she believes make the best rag rugs. She is interested in fabric quality more than color. "If I find something at the resale shop that is faded but in good condition, then I dye it. I don't think about color while I'm in the resale shop."

Judy is so well-known for her rugs in northeast Iowa that every year three church circles bring her bushel baskets filled with balls of fabric they have cut, torn, and sewed together into strips and then rolled. Judy simply weaves the balls into rugs that they sell at their bazaars.

It takes her about an hour and a half to weave each kitchen sink–sized rug and another half hour to tie the ends. It takes her a day to warp the loom.

Judy can't really explain what makes her rugs distinct and unusual. "I start with a ball and find another ball. I have a color sense," she says.

She bought her sixty-year-old, forty-four-inch-wide loom, manufactured by the Newcomb Loom Company of Davenport, Iowa, about twenty years ago. The loom had been forgotten in someone's old shed. Later, she found a second loom.

Not only does Judy like partaking in an early American folk art, she also likes continuing a craft handed down from an era when nothing was thrown away. "I got interested when I started weaving myself. I like the fact that I can recycle things. I sew and enjoy fabrics."

Judy stops weaving the rug and walks to the barnyard on a hill overlooking farms beyond. At one barn she is greeted by eighteen Angora goats. At the other barn twenty-nine sheep trot toward her. The friendly one she bottle-fed for weeks pushes through the others toward her. Judy and the baaing sheep have an understandable bond.

During lambing season in the brittle cold of March and April, Judy got up every four hours to care for these animals. "I'm always down there checking. I have to be there watching, making sure they are nursing. If there are problems, I have to separate them. Sometimes the firstborn will wander off with other sheep and get lost. It's hard to go out when it's way below zero, and everything is frozen."

The sheep and goats became a part of her life after she bought her first regular weaving loom and started making pillows, tapestries, runners, and yardage for clothes. Then she decided to raise sheep and goats for their wool and mohair. She has a new and an old spinning wheel, a further tie to the early 1900s.

The weaving of fabric and rugs is interspersed between responsibilities that go with being a modern day farmwife. Her chores are unlike those her mother knew. Judy does work equal to what her husband does. "More neighbors helped then," she recalls. "Nowadays, we have more land and bigger machinery. We have more critters to raise and lots of hogs. We couldn't survive on the small numbers of the past. We have to get larger scale. Now the husband and wife do the work, or if I didn't do it, we'd have to hire a hired man. So now lots of modern farmwives run the tractors.

"We have to work together. We hay together. It takes two of us to do it. During the summer I run the chopper, and he unloads the hay. In the spring I help put in crops. I run the tractor. I don't spend a whole lot of time weaving then—it's more in the winter. Sometimes we work together on livestock."

Chuck—tall, laid-back, and in charge of the hog operation on the farm (one thousand farrow-to-finish a year)—says it plainly. "We're partners."

Judy, who gives spinning and weaving demonstrations at the Vesterheim Museum, is so at home on the farm that she only goes into town once a week. "I go into town with a list. It takes a half day if I go to town. I buy groceries, feed and medicine for the livestock. ..."

And she hurries back down the gravel roads past Big Canoe Lutheran Church to the turn-of-the-century life she is trying to replicate. At each door are rag rugs that she made. There is a garden, chickens, sheep—and goats.

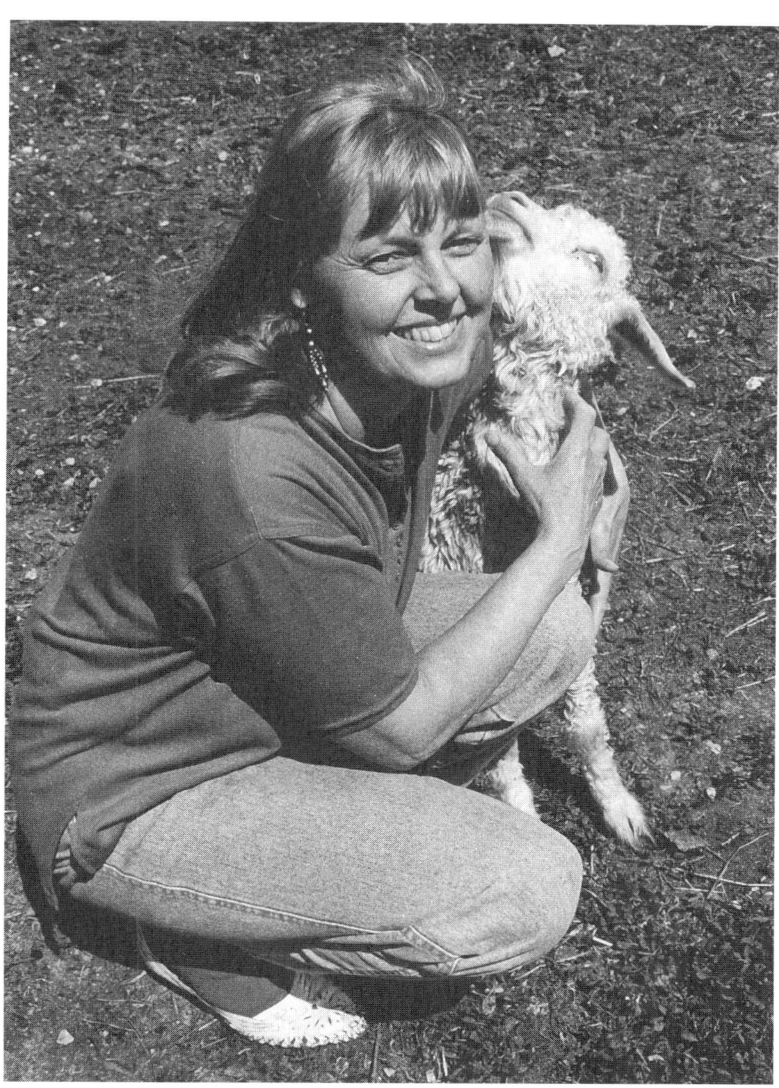

*Judy raises Angora
goats and sheep on her
hilltop farm.*

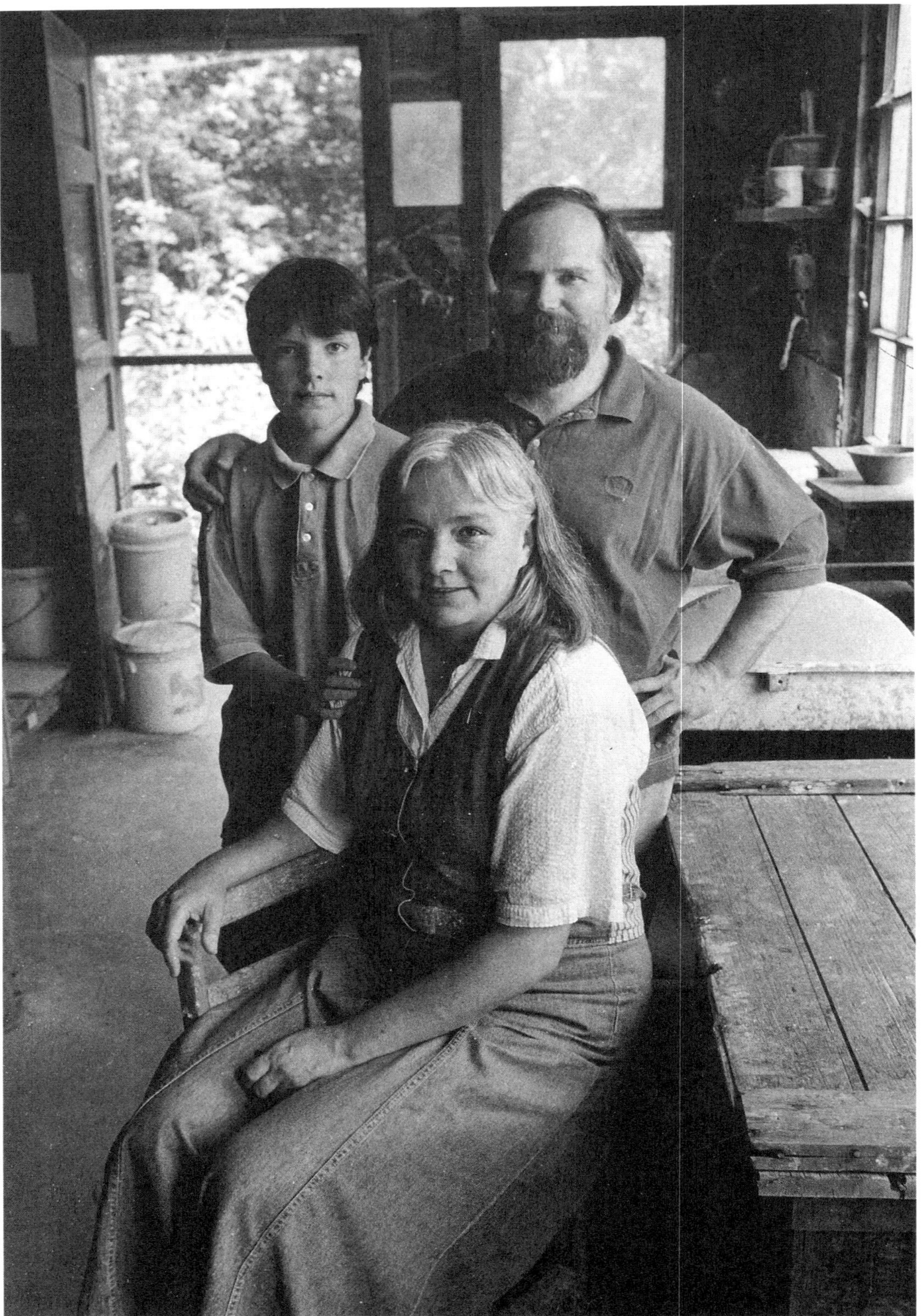

RUSS AND JACKIE LECKBAND

Russ and Jackie Leck-band, with son, Jesse: "The ware that we produce is primarily traditional kitchenware. The forms are hardy and generous, with a focus on sturdy function. The stoneware and occasional porcelain are made by hand on a potter's wheel. After a suitable amount of drying, the ware is decorated by us with a variety of slips in cobalt blue, brown, or green. Some designs are one of a kind; others are inspired by traditional early American pieces. The dry pottery is then stacked in a kiln and fired to final heat around 2,300 Fahrenheit."

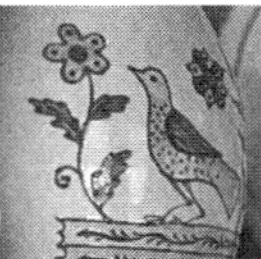Down a wooded gravel road near Earlham, a little over a mile from the busy interstate, is Bear Creek Meeting House and, just beyond, the home and studio of potter Russell Leckband and his folk artist wife, Jackie. They live and work in the nineteenth-century style. They collect rainwater off the roof, enjoy the warmth of a woodstove, and listen to the warblers and wrens from their outdoor toilet. They teach their son, Jesse, fourteen, at home.

Living a simple life close to nature is what the Leckbands choose. This reverence for the past is very much a part of Russ's pottery, which is created in the nineteenth-century stoneware tradition—a tradition that died out at the turn of the century. "We try to live in nature," he allows. "Sometimes it's not simple to do. We have a son dragging us kicking and screaming into the twentieth century."

Their wooded eleven acres is a sanctuary, protected from the rest of the world by wildflowers, oaks, and basswoods, similar to what Iowa's early settlers saw. This haven is part of an old-fashioned close-knit Quaker community where a neighbor is a neighbor in the true sense. "Our immediate neighbors are really supportive of each other," Jackie explains. "I'm not sure we could do as well in other places."

Russ, whose dark red beard and classic features suggest a pioneer, sits on a stool in the glass and wood studio he built from salvaged materials, sometimes with the help of neighbors. "If we had moved twenty years ago one mile farther in either direction, we wouldn't have been as closely connected," he says. "I don't know what would have happened, but our lives would have been a lot different." Jackie agrees. She appears to ingest constantly the loveliness from everything around her.

Russ recollects when a "friend of a friend" told them this house was for rent because the owner, also a potter, had moved to Kentucky. "We came to pay the rent to the owner's mother, a strong Quaker. She helped us get involved in the community, and eventually we bought the house."

Leckband was raised to respect hard work while growing up on the edge of Des Moines. He dished up ice cream, delivered papers, and made popcorn at the Val Air Ballroom. He didn't discover pottery until his last semesters at Northwest Missouri State University, when he filled up his schedule with ceramics classes.

After college in 1974 he took a job as a farmhand at Living History Farms, an open-air agricultural museum in Des Moines where he shoveled manure and fixed fences. About that time a potter was hired at the farms, and Russ became his apprentice. He had that position a year and a half, until the potter moved on. Russ took his place.

"I wasn't that good after a year of ceramics in college and one and a half years as an apprentice," he admits. "When you have two hundred to three hundred people coming through a day wanting to see pottery being made, maybe you don't make technically the best pots, but you make them look like pottery.

"It was a production pottery situation depending on the size of the piece—three or four dozen to a hundred per day. The pots eventually were fired in a kiln large enough to hold about one thousand pieces. When there were enough pieces ready for the kiln, Jackie's mother, Marge Mable, who owns the store Folkart in West Des Moines, would come out and decorate the pots." (See Chap. 15.)

Russ was the potter at Living History Farms for eighteen years. It was here that he noticed Jackie when she was a hostess in the farm's log cabin. "I was living in a tepee in the horse pasture," he remembers. They had what she calls a "summer courtship," married, and moved to the little town of Commerce, Iowa, where they had no running water or electricity. "I thought it was great," he recalls. "There was no roof in the tepee. I had a roof."

At Living History Farms he had the security of a small salary and money from selling his pots. As part of his job his materials were provided. He and Jackie occasionally discussed someday having their own studio—about going out on their own. "It was one of those things. Someday we wanted a perfect studio. We didn't want to do it until we had the right conditions. You want everything ready."

That time came sooner than they expected. One day in 1991, he lost his job over a political stand he took regarding the commission of some pots. "The job left before I was ready to build a shop," Russ recalls. "I had to build anyway. Life's like that. ... Sometimes you get little nudges and pushes that send you on a different path than you wanted to go on."

A smile breaks into this sequence when he remembers the day that changed his life. He went out in Marge's pontoon boat with her and his mother. Marge listened to the story and said, "What a wonderful opportunity."

"We knew deep down that it was something we needed to do and wanted to do," Jackie remembers. "But it was the dark night of the soul time." They weren't going back to a tepee because they already had paid for their land and house.

Jackie gave up the living room in their small rustic house—she thought temporarily—so Russ could move in his potter's wheel and continue to make pots until the studio was built. Temporarily became four years. She remembers how it was. "We did it bit by bit when we could pay for it. It's a bit-by-bit building. Most bankers don't lend. ... They say, 'You want to use old materials?' We didn't sleep for weeks."

That first fall on their own, they looked forward to the Covered Bridge Festival in Winterset, where they hoped to sell enough pots to build up some savings. Just before the festival they loaded and fired up a kiln they had owned for twenty-five years and used only occasionally. It was fired with wood and fuel oil.

"The firing ended late at night," Russ remembers. "I went to bed. Jackie was doing something and went out, looked in the kiln, and told me something was wrong. I went out and looked at the kiln, and the whole kiln was in flames."

Russ tried to put the fire out with an extinguisher, but the rubber hose for the oil had melted near the kiln and spewed oil in front of the kiln. The shed burned down. "The fire department wanted to put out the glowing kiln. I told them not to put out the kiln."

He remembers his foreboding, his dread to look into the kiln. "If we get anything out of this, we'll be happy," he remembers. "For some reason pots out of that load were the best ever. Maybe it was the water vapor. They had an iridescence. That was the ceremonial end to that kiln."

Now he uses electric kilns in his studio, and he borrows a wood kiln from friends. He looks at the pile of wood in front of the studio and thinks about having a large wood- or gas-fired kiln. "This is the dream," he says.

Russ's pottery, like the way he and Jackie live, is based on a

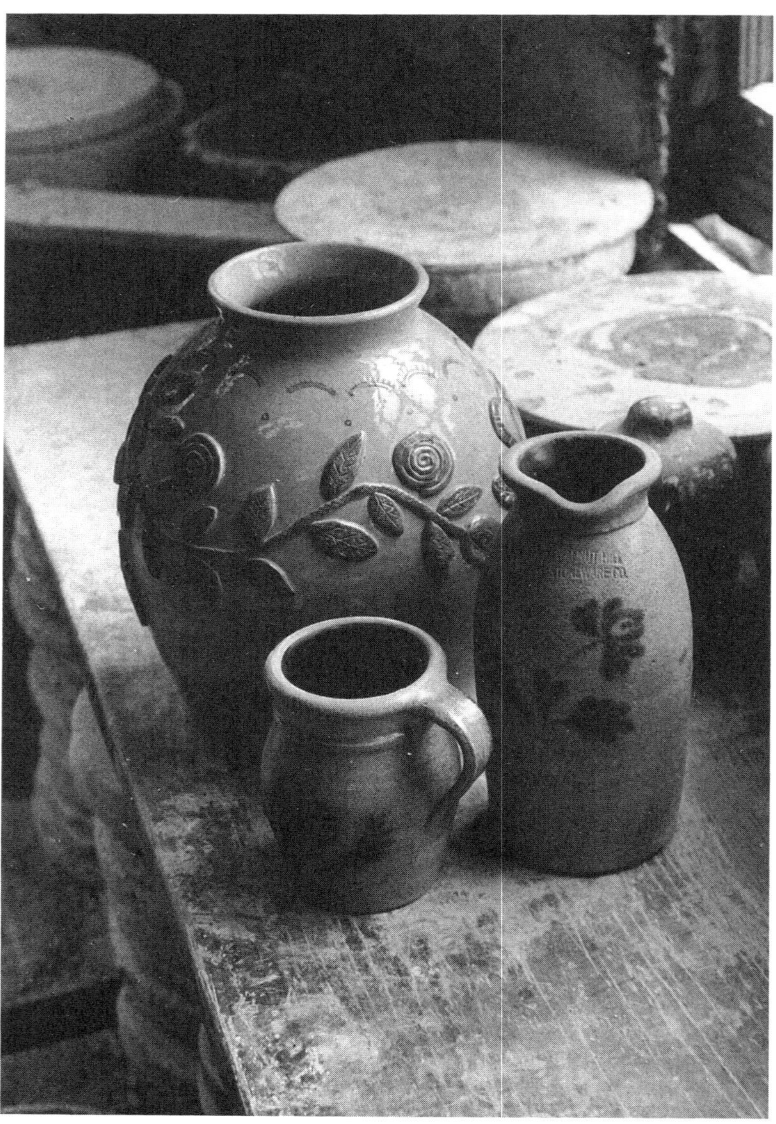

Leckband pots have a nineteenth-century feel to them.

respect for tradition. "It goes back to that sense of community. Historically, potters were creating useful things for the community. That defined their culture. The culture from the last century has gotten away from local needs." Russ's pottery exemplifies basic kitchenware that was once used for everyday living—storage jars, pie plates, mugs, jugs, and crocks.

"I think handmade pottery is still resilient," he adds. "The tradition is really resilient. Even in our technological age, people respect handmade things more. A lot of people can go three days and not be around anything handmade."

In the bright studio, with windows that bring the woods in-

82   IOWA FOLK ARTISTS

doors, is an electric wheel for throwing and trimming and a treader wheel for trimming and decorations. He uses commercial stoneware clay and a basic, simple clear glaze similar to that used in big pottery factories like Red Wing and Monmouth at the turn of the century.

Why he specializes in nineteenth-century stoneware is evident—clues pile up one on top of the other. "It was a crossroads," he says. "Being a student in the early '70s, a product of the back-to-the-land idea, combined with opportunities at the Living History Farms and an interest in history. It all fit together."

Although they do some pottery stamped with minimal designs to pay the bills, much of it Jackie decorates simply in the nineteenth-century tradition. She works at a small counter underneath a window. Quietly, she points out her "inspiration" shelf, which holds modest objects that have particular meaning for her. A book is opened to "Rest and Be Thankful." Written in pencil is the verse "Look for the sacred in the ordinary." There's a verse from Robert Frost. "My object in life is to unite my avocation and my vocation." There's an old tobacco tin, in which her dad kept nails, and a china cup that was her grandmother's. She picks up a simple pewter top. "It's such a wonderful design." She holds it as if it were a fragile glass figurine.

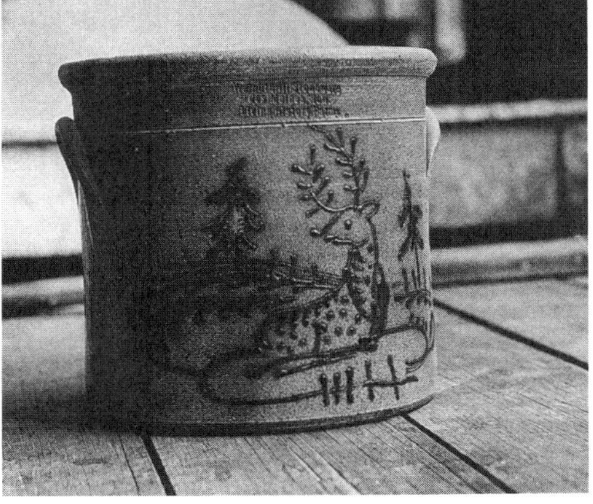

A simple pot is uniquely decorated by Jackie.

These objects encourage the designs she puts on pottery. Not surprisingly, "'tis a gift to be simple, 'tis a gift to be free" is painted on several crocks.

She claims Russ just hands his finished pots over to her. "He never says anything." She looks at the pot and thinks, "What can I put on his pot to enhance it?" She picks up a crock and points out the pieces of clay she applied to the pot. This came from her love of textiles.

It's not unusual for Russ to work from 9 a.m. until 1 or 2 a.m. Long hours. "If an order needs to be done and the kiln loaded, we need to decorate and glaze pots until the kiln is filled."

The Quaker influence in both their day-to-day living and in their work is evident. They are active in the traditional Bear

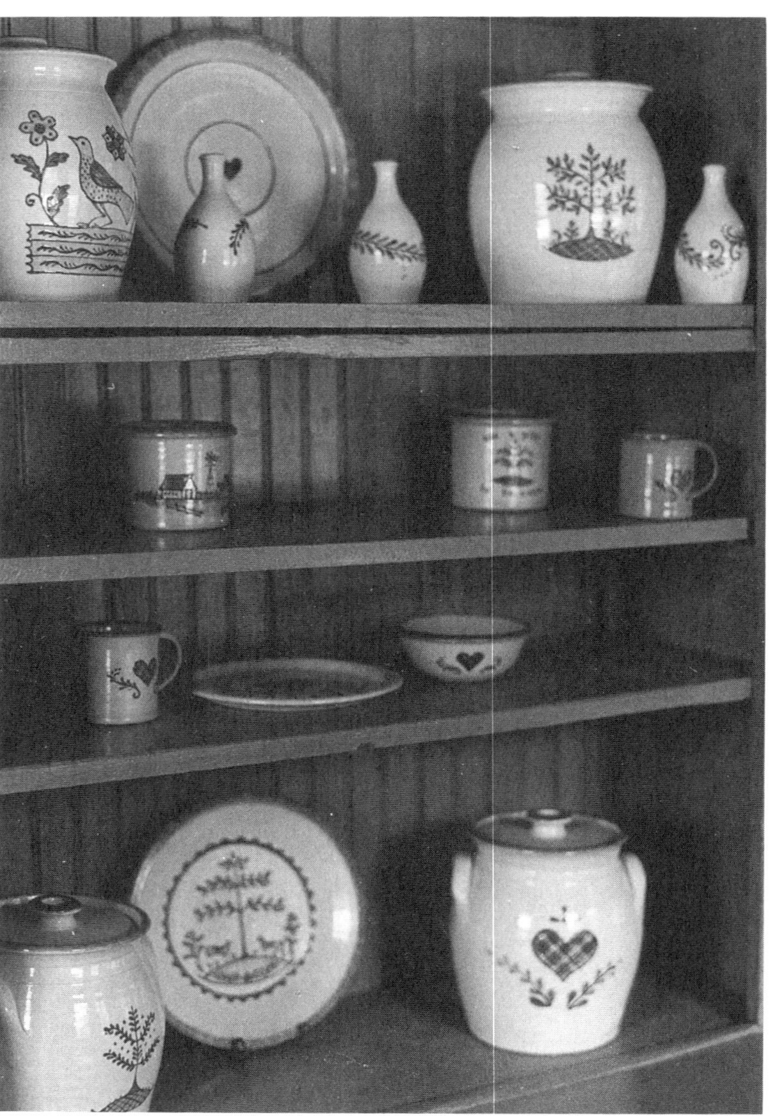

Creek Meeting House, which has a "silent service." "They
have different testimonies. One of their testimonies—the testimony of simplicity—fits in with our lifestyle," Russ explains.
"They also have a peace testimony. We do a lot with peace
and social concerns." Jackie adds in a quiet and unusually sincere way, "Quakers look for God in everyone."

Russ continues, "Every part of life is a balance. We're not
going to say we're not going to enjoy those parts of civilization
that can be useful." (He notes that they have bought a com-
puter.)

The way their life is set up, there is little time for recreation.

                                    IOWA FOLK ARTISTS

"Our social agenda is very much dictated by what the kiln is doing. If I leave here and go to Des Moines, I'm still wondering what I'll do to get back to see the kiln. It only takes one-half to one hour to ruin everything in a load."

Jackie looks fondly at Russ as if he knows what she is about to say and is waiting for approval. "I've said, 'Oh, it won't matter.' Oops ... people wanting their plate the next day are not so happy."

They both teach Jesse, a handsome, serious, brown-haired teenager, at home. Russ was a history major, so he concentrates on that area. As a family they go on field trips to the capitol, to ethnic food stores. "We always wanted to do home schooling, so we thought this is a good time. It's life's skills," he says. "It's everywhere—walking out to the pond, cooking," Jackie observes.

It is weeks before the Iowa State Fair, but Russ is laboring late hours to build up his inventory. This ten-day event brings in one-fourth to one-third of the Leckbands' annual income. He takes three truckloads of pottery and equipment to the fair before it ever begins. At the giant fair he will not only sell his pots but will also demonstrate the art. "It really makes a connection with the people we sell to," he says. It also promotes an interest in nineteenth-century–style stoneware, which helps to sustain the art.

Russ looks tired while he takes a few hours off. "I'm immensely amazed I'm allowed to be able to do this for a living," he thinks out loud. "Some days, I wonder if I'll ever be found out and have to get a proper job. When you're doing something like this, you're grateful if you're allowed to do it. We're not people who sit down with a business plan—to go into it and operate five or six years. We operate on faith and abundance."

He estimates there are only twenty-five potters in Iowa making their living from pottery. "I know twenty potters who had to quit because, with a family, it was too much." Russ hopes they can stay local.

Jackie looks lovingly toward Russ. "We made a choice to live in this way—to live simply."

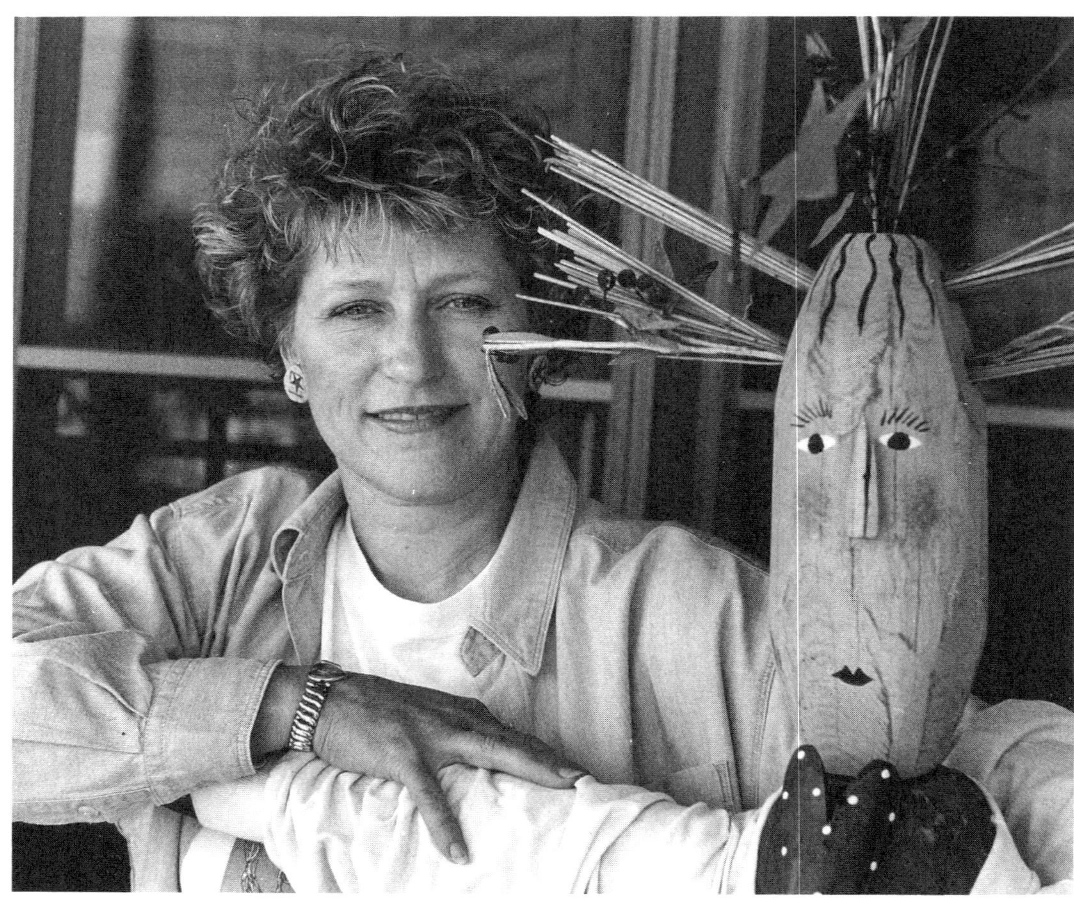

Pam Dyer Walters: "I start with an untreated pine post. Posts are in various sizes and shapes. It is cut to length, then carved and shaped on the band saw and sander. Everything is then hand-painted and hand-sanded and antiqued to look old. Finally I hand-detail paint and assemble. No two figures are exactly alike."

PAM DYER WALTERS

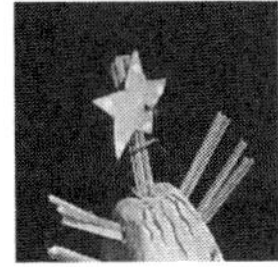 It is 2 a.m. The phone is not ringing. No one is hollering, "Mom." Pam Dyer Walters, vivacious and industrious mother of three, is in her basement workshop holding a ten-pound post, using a band saw to shape it into an angel. Dressed in paint-covered sweats, she works as proficiently as a master carpenter, ignoring the weight of the posts that might overwhelm the mightier. She shapes the edges of the angel with a band saw, then deftly gives it character by scuffing it with the sander.

This angel has a large body, a tiny head. Her name is "Beulah." She is named for the late Beulah Schultz, a friend's grandmother who had a large back. "She was a wonderful, caring person," Pam remembers. "Her body was not big enough to carry all the love she had."

"Beulah" is one of a series of Santas, Uncle Sams, and angels Pam sculpts from crude posts, all named for neighbors and friends—mostly in her town of Winterset—that she admires. There's "Neil," a round-bellied snowman named for Neil Hampton, her children's godfather, who is "slightly big around the middle." ("You exaggerate some feature. You hope their feelings are not hurt.") Marianne Fons, a friend Pam quilts with, is immortalized as "Marianne," who wears her signature felt jacket. "Frances" is in honor of Frances Wight, local basketmaker, who makes the wreaths for Pam's figures. "Jo Ellen" is a token of gratitude for Jo Ellen Fewerke, a friend since kindergarten. "Fonda" was created in honor of former hairdresser Fonda Bass, an old friend and confidante.

Pam's father, Gordon Marquardt, is recreated as "Gordon," an angel holding a fishing pole and rake. "He symbolizes the years I was a single mom and he'd help. I'd say, 'I need to rake the leaves.' My dad pitched in and helped me do anything and everything."

Her figures have an uncomplicated, primitive charm that speaks to people. Perhaps this is because Pam's elementary school teacher told her she couldn't draw, and that was the end of her art training. "I never took another art class, and I still can't draw," says Pam. "I try to go back and think like a child. I don't worry if the feet don't match. I don't worry about proportions."

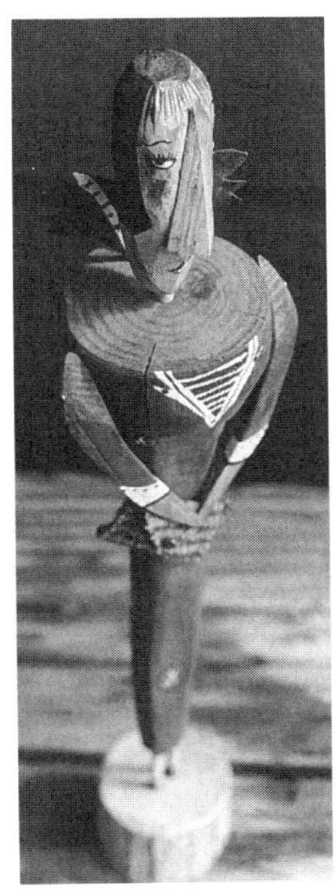

"Sandra," one of Dyer's angels named for a friend.

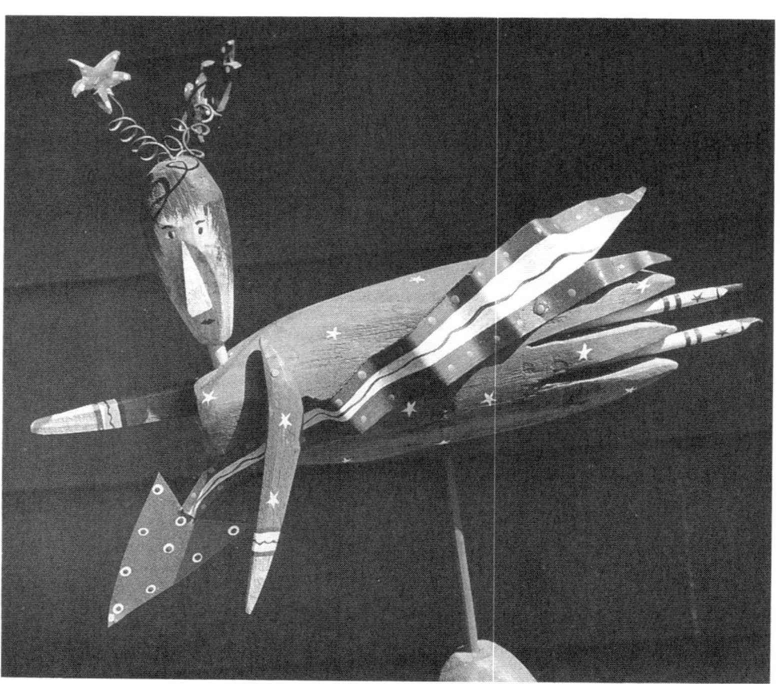

She still doesn't. It's the delightful mismatch of proportions, the out-of-context arms and legs, the message that no one is perfect, that imperfect is all right, that endears her figures to people. In folk art stores, where her folks—usually painted in reds, blues, and greens—are carried, customers affectionately refer to them as "Pam Dyers," as if they actually know Pam.

Pam, a naturally friendly, easy-to-know person, attended high school in Adel and then went to a cosmetology school. She married and had a daughter, Amanda. Amanda was six when Emily was born prematurely. "We couldn't pay medical bills without extra income," she recalls. "I started making simple things—hearts that I could stencil, flatware." She planned to participate in one Covered Bridge Festival, an annual event in Winterset, the Madison County seat.

The few hearts led to more, larger hearts, for five years. "I didn't plan on staying in business. Then I started using the money to work on our old house."

This drive was rooted in her childhood. "As a child I worked to stay busy. I was raised the way to get things was to work for them. There were no handouts."

When she started making Santas and angels, her former husband cut pieces out for her with saws. Finally, he said to

IOWA FOLK ARTISTS

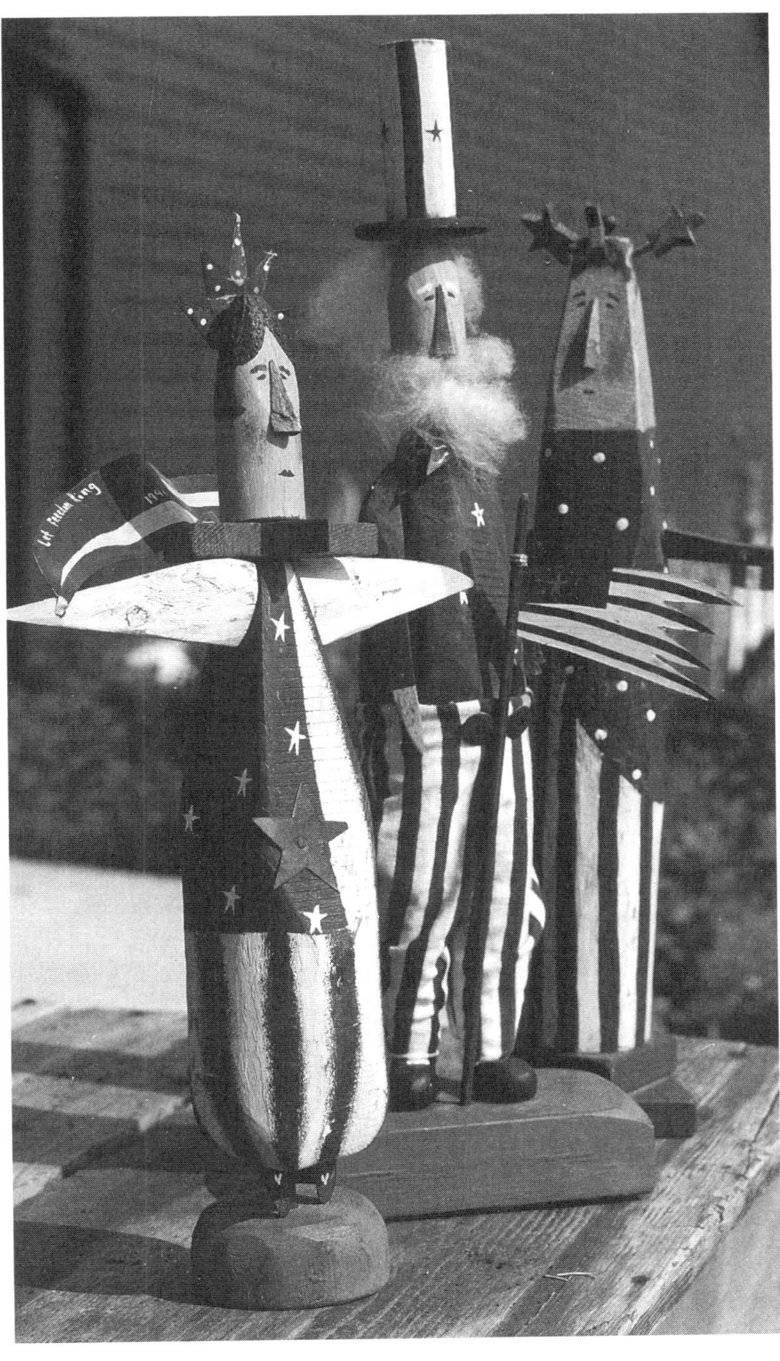

Ms. Liberty, Uncle Sam, and Little Liberty stand on Pam's back porch.

her, "I already have a job, and I don't want to come home and work all night too." He showed her how to use a band saw and radial arm saw.

Pam took to the saws as if she had picked up an embroidery needle. "The band saw was like using a sewing machine—but

PAM DYER WALTERS

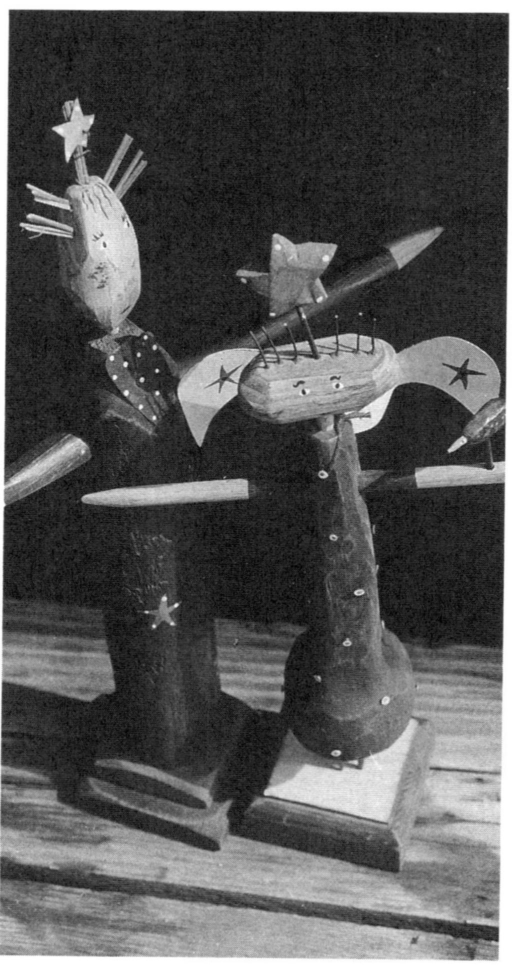

"Pam" and "Jo Ellen."

you can cut your finger off." She experimented freely with the saw. She tried making Santas. "In a couple of years I started carving with the saw. I'd hold the wood at different angles and pull it through."

Though all the "Beulahs" or all the "Weary Santas" may be similar, each is different in expression or size or shape. Each face is hand-painted, individual. Nothing is stenciled. "The wood itself has so much character. Nothing of mine is the same. No two posts are the same. Some people might criticize because they're not perfect. My feeling is there's little in this world that is perfect. We're all unique individuals."

It is the I-can-take-on-anything attitude that helped Pam vault difficult hurdles in her life. There was a divorce, and in 1990 she was a single parent raising Amanda, twelve, Emily, seven, and Molly, two.

To supplement child support, she worked evenings part time in a beauty shop four blocks from the house. She left Amanda in charge. One night, Amanda called and told her that Emily had hurt herself. "Emily fell and wouldn't stop crying. I was the only one working and couldn't leave. It turned out she had a broken leg. I felt badly. She was in pain, and I wasn't there. I made the decision to just do my art—to work longer hours and make it go.

"I sent pieces to the Museum of American Folk Art Shop, and they liked my stuff. They say when God shuts the door he opens a window. It was like twenty windows were opened. It gave me the recognition and credentials I needed. It still meant working many, many hours."

This change from the security of a regular salary to irregular income meant keeping expenses basic. "It was tough. I had house payments, utilities, groceries, and child care expenses. If I had a doctor or dentist's bill, I paid in installments. There were times I couldn't pay $56 to have my teeth cleaned.

"The first year I'd go to bed crying and praying God would

give me the strength to keep up. By the second year I knew I'd be okay. Anytime I didn't have to be busy with my kids, I was working."

Pam's dad, with his no-work-is-too-much attitude, has been a major influence on Pam. Growing up, she watched him work long hours to support the family. Now he works hard to help her. "He was an auto mechanic. It goes back to working with your hands. He got base pay. If he worked more, he got a bonus, so he worked his whole life 150 percent. Sometimes I'll look over at my dad, who is working, and say, 'No one's paying a bonus. Slow down.'" She is momentarily pensive. "I'm getting to know my father a lot better than I ever did."

She knew Christmas wouldn't be the same the first year she created folk art full time, so instead of gifts, she gave the children a March vacation. She saw an advertisement for dogsledding in Montana. "I called and found I could get there on Amtrack. I didn't have a credit card to rent a car. I told them I'd pay when I got there."

So she and the girls drove to Minneapolis, got on Amtrack, traveled twenty-four hours, went dogsledding one day, skiing another, and turned around and came back. "That was all I could afford, but it was wonderful. My girls will never forget that trip."

By the next year she had done well enough that she flew the girls to Arizona and drove through the parks there for eight days. She also had enough money to strip and repaint the woodwork in the house and to put in a new sidewalk.

Later, Pam met and married Stephen Walters, a lawyer in Winterset. For a while they lived in Pam's turn-of-the-century house on Court Avenue. Then together they designed and built a barn-red clapboard colonial house across from cornfields, almost out of town. Pam looks around the spacious rooms of the house, which she has decorated like an old farmhouse, with quilts and embroideries. All of the bricks used in the house are from the Adel brick factory where her grandfather worked. "One of the wonderful things I've learned is knowing I can take care of myself and the kids. I have the knowledge of knowing I can do it."

The new house was easy to plan "when you know how much space you need to make cookies," she explains. The basement studio is also spacious enough to hold her band saw, chain saw, drill press, router, and sander. The garage sometimes holds as many as 350 untreated pine posts from the Adel lumberyard.

"Walter," a happy snowman, is named for Stephen. One night while they were dating, Stephen stopped in a store and bought a bunch of socks. When Pam asked him what he was going to do with his old socks, he told her he would use them for rags. That was the challenge Pam needed. The socks were transformed into jackets for "Walter."

Out the back door of their house are gardens bursting with flowers. This takes Pam back to tender thoughts of her great-grandmother who lived on two lots in Van Meter, Iowa. One lot was for the house and the other for the garden. Pam believes that not only her love of gardens but also her sense of design were handed down from this great-grandmother. "She was also a quilter. She had a little, tiny house, but there was a quilt frame in the living room and, outside, flowers all over." Pam never forgot this.

This great-grandmother's daughter, Pam's grandmother, taught Pam embroidery, cross-stitchery, knitting, and crocheting. Pam had a talent for sewing and by ninth grade was doing tailoring in classes. "The need to create was always there."

She talks about her great-grandmother and grandmother almost as if they're in the room with her. "The older I get, the more I get like my grandma and great-grandma. My parents don't know how I got this. My mom can't thread a sewing machine. It must have been hard for them to raise someone so different."

It is obvious when Pam talks about this great-grandmother, who lived to be ninety-seven, that she was a significant person in her life. "Amanda took custard pudding from the pharmacy snack bar to the nursing home every day and fed her," Pam reminisces.

"She has been a determining factor of who I am today," Pam says, passing chocolate chip cookies that she and the girls have just made in their large and homey kitchen.

She wants to talk more about her great-grandmother, as if she has just found the right word in a crossword puzzle. "I'm starting to understand what I think was so strange about her. I just didn't understand why she liked so many flowers. It was the only place I went with a quilting frame. I have a whole floor devoted to creating from wood and tin. She'd take scraps of cloth and create wonderful quilts."

For Pam, passing on the legacy handed down by her great-grandmother and grandmother is important to her. She taught twenty Brownies to quilt. "What I love most is when I go to Molly's class. I love children's art. It is true-true folk art. Tell them to draw a Santa and reindeer—they don't think about whether the head is proportional."

When she creates something new, Pam puts it out for her daughters to criticize first. "Once I put something out in the bathroom, and Amanda said, 'Mom, your head does weird things at 3 a.m.'

"When I'm creating, I look at shapes—at absolutely everything. I experiment with what a line here will do and what a line there will do. Today, I'm noticing the shape of things with the wind blowing. I don't know if it's conscious. ... It's a feel. It's a feeling."

She returns to thoughts of the teacher who, a long time ago, almost crushed her talent. "I don't think I ever challenged her. I don't have to sit down and draw the house across the street to be an artist. My clay work in elementary grades was great.

"Maybe if she'd said, 'You're a good artist, but better at free form.' I guess you don't need to draw to be an artist."

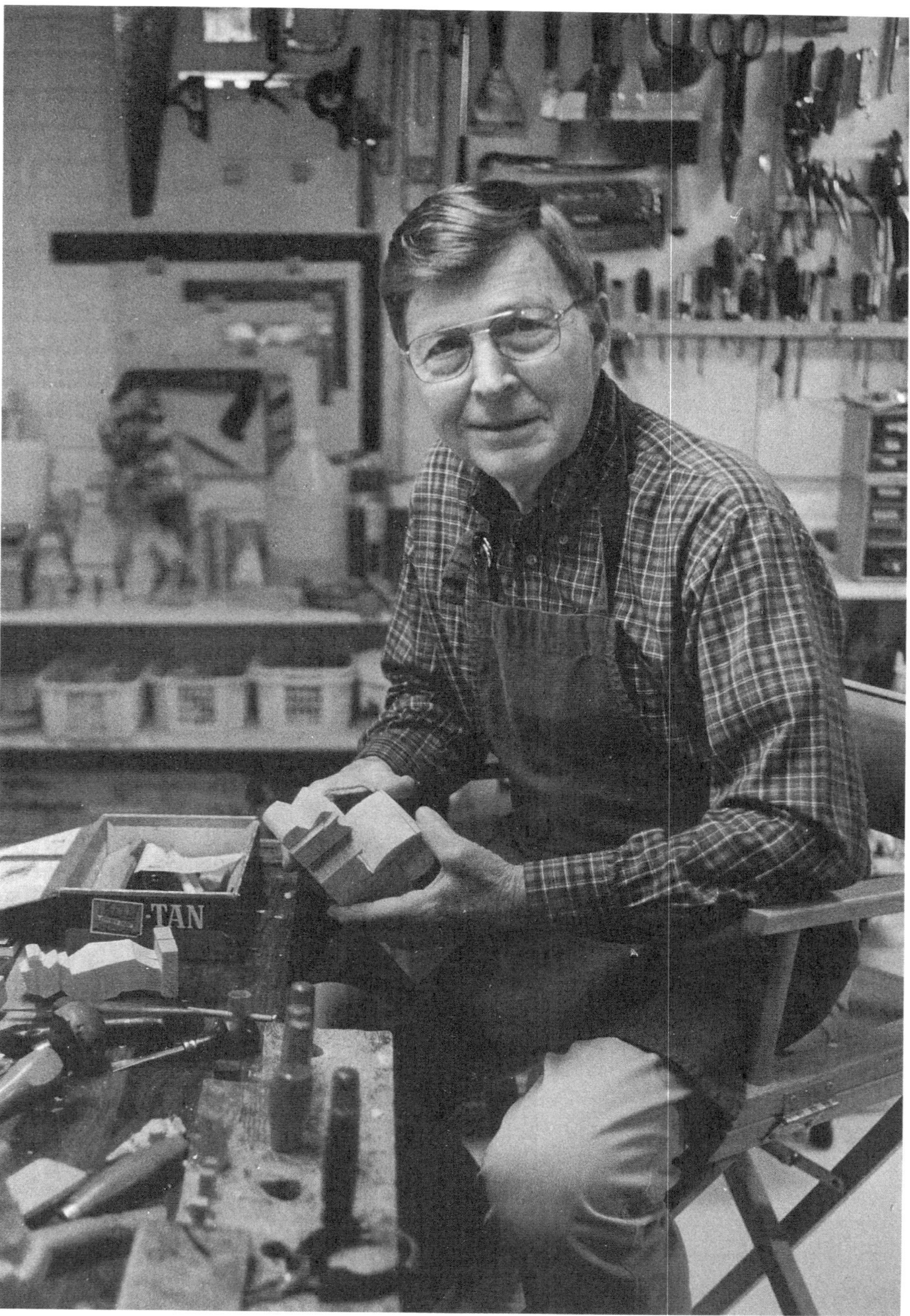

BILL WARRICK

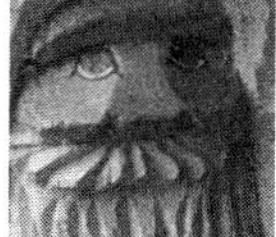

By the time carver Bill Warrick was a teenager in Brazil, Indiana, he had experienced more occupations than most people ever encounter. He had seen his father, a coal miner, come home filthy after working a twelve-hour day in the mines and clean up in a washtub. On weekends he had sat beside his father in the upstairs of a concessions stand while he earned extra money playing drums in a concert band.

His dad died at age fifty-three with a lung disorder precipitated by mining. Suddenly, Bill, the youngest of five, had to work to pay his own day-to-day expenses. He started a series of before- and after-school jobs. He delivered papers, whipped up malts in a soda fountain, made casket sprays in a flower shop, and set pins in a bowling alley. For no pay he helped his mother, a split-shift cook and dishwasher, in a restaurant late at night so she could leave earlier.

At seventeen he left the coal-mining town for the security of the navy. "My first in-the-house bathroom was when I went into the navy," he recalls. When the war ended, he worked as an electrician's apprentice and later as a dress cutter in a garment company.

He found job security by age twenty-two, when he settled on a career as an engineer at John Deere in Des Moines. But the experience of knowing, at an impressionable age, the different ways people live and work was imprinted on his memory. This, perhaps, explains why his carvings convey such empathy and compassion for occupations.

Bill admits that his carvings are influenced by what people do for a living. "I lean more heavily toward life's occupations. I've carved a pilot, a surgeon, a doctor, nurses, farmers, painters. There's a lot of interest in it. I'm sure experiences I had growing up contributed to what comes out in my carving."

After his father's death he turned to the Boy Scouts in his hometown for the fellowship that he yearned. The Boy Scouts not only gave him the companionship that he wanted but also experiences that generated his interest in carving, his love of wood. Through the scouts he learned to appreciate nature, "and wood is a living fiber," he points out. "I always had a knife and a piece of wood in my hand when I was in the country."

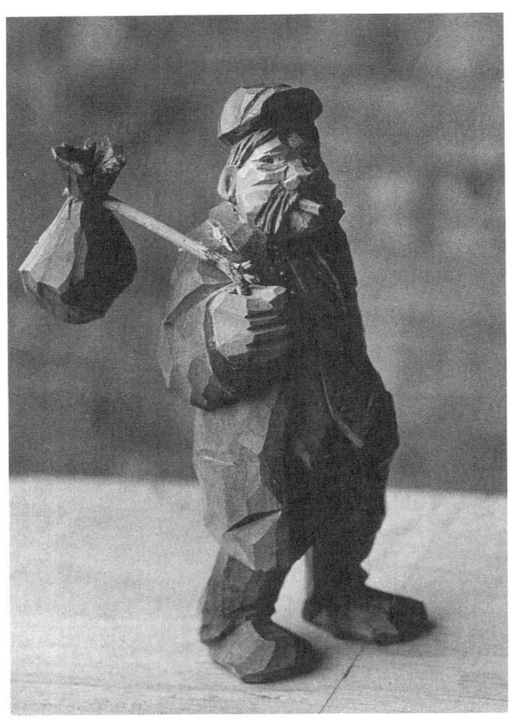

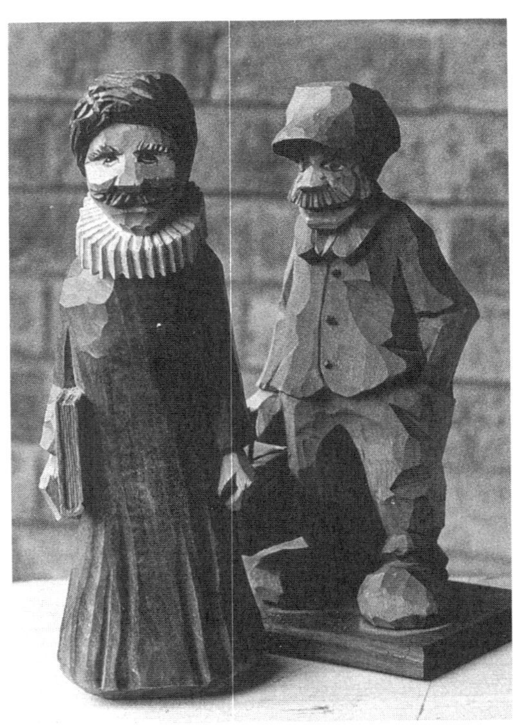

One scout outing remains poignant in his memory. "All of us carried a knife. Our scoutmaster had us all hike into the timber. We were met with a huge pot of baked beans and paper plates. There were no utensils. If we wanted to eat, we had to carve our own utensils. I ate. I carved a spoon out of a stick. Some of the kids didn't eat because they couldn't carve. The idea was to make you know you could be self-sufficient."

Bill, who is thin and has an unwithered complexion, sits in the comfortable living room of a West Des Moines condominium. He looks younger than his seventy-two years. He is intelligent, soft-spoken in an assertive way. Only the glasses hint at his age. Doris, his devoted wife, also has the healthy, well-cared-for look of someone much younger. They met at a United Service Organizations dance when he was a cadet stationed in Ottumwa during the war, and they married a year later. She was born in Chillicothe, Iowa, and fifty-one years ago, she brought to their marriage a strong family and rural upbringing that Bill had missed. Since then, they have worked through life almost in tandem.

Thoughts of carving were put aside for the thirty-five years Bill worked at John Deere. "I was using my mind in another way," he remembers. "I had a large budget I was responsible for. But I've always been creative. Even when I worked on weekends, I was delving into some creative and artistic endeavors. I did sterling silver jewelry and stained glass."

While visiting Switzerland in 1976, he bought a wood-carving set, "brought it home, put it in a drawer, and forgot about it until 1982. I knew I had it." Then, through some "over-the-fence talk," he was invited to a meeting of the Mid-Iowa Woodcarvers Club. He was intrigued and got the tools out. As it turned out, he retired one month and was carving the next.

"The club would have demonstrations. The first piece I carved was a duck because that's what they were demonstrating. I tried relief carving because so many were carving ducks, and I wanted to do something different. I enjoyed that."

One weekend in 1984, Harley Refsal (Chapter 1), the carver from Decorah who is bringing flat plane carving back in both Norway and America, conducted a workshop for the group. Warrick was captivated. "The first piece he carved was a gnome. I liked the minimal number of cuts to achieve a fea-

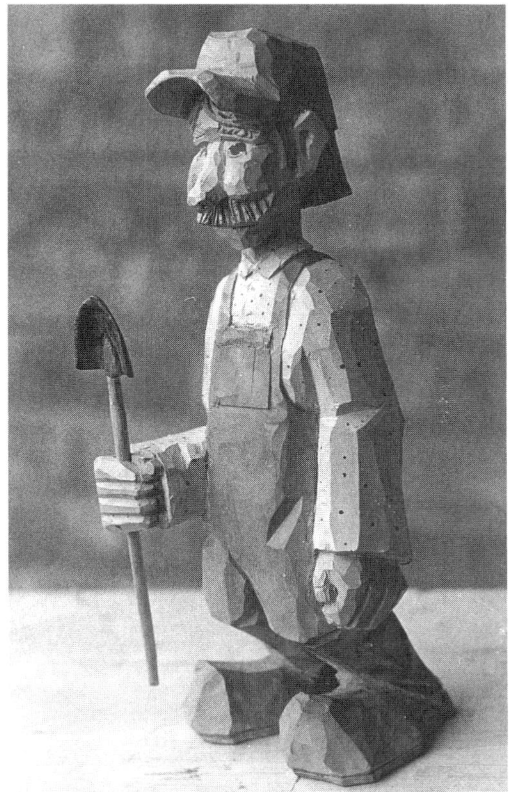

Farmers are favorite subjects of Bill's.

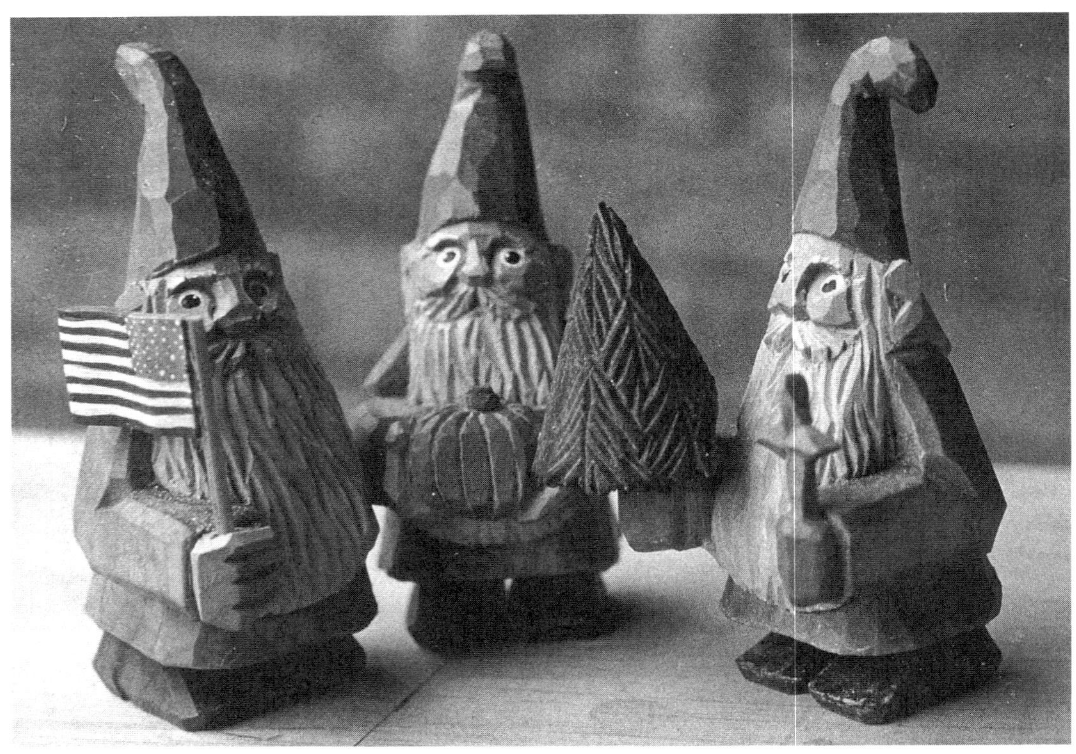

ture—the challenge to see how few cuts were necessary to get a feature. We just got other books and adapted ideas to that style of carving."

Five years later, Warrick noted an opportunity to receive a grant for folk art in the Iowa Arts Council Newsletter. His age, sixty-two, didn't deter him. He applied and was given a grant sponsored jointly by the Iowa Arts Council and the National Endowment for the Arts. He asked Harley if he could apprentice with him. Harley agreed, so one weekend a month for a year, Bill drove to Decorah to study.

Before working with Harley, Bill was self-taught. Now he considers himself "half self-taught." "The apprenticeship was a big boost. It gave me confidence and enthusiasm. Harley broke the ice for me to experiment with drawing and tools."

Bill is up at 6 a.m. and carves from 8 a.m. to noon in his basement workshop. Before he carves an object, he makes sketches. His medium is basswood, which he buys in Dayton, Iowa. To cut out the shapes of his characters, he uses a band saw. For small pieces he uses a scroll saw.

His main tool is a knife that he bought in Mora, Sweden. If it gets dull, he has four others from which to choose. He has

                                   IOWA FOLK ARTISTS

immortalized in wood a series of workers—the bespeckled painter carrying a bucket, the lawyer holding a briefcase, the cowboy wearing hat and kerchief, and the farmer grasping the suspenders of his coveralls. He has created an aviator, a surgeon gripping a surgical clamp, and a fisherman holding a fishing pole. The faces are serious, yet happy, and almost real.

His gnomes are another forte. A gnome was the first piece he saw Harley carve, and something about the dwarf of folklore enchanted him. "I modified the design. Something told me there should be one for every month." So his gnomes ski in January and carry a heart in February, a shamrock in March, and a yellow umbrella in April. They hold a fish or flag in July, an apple in September, and a pumpkin in October. His gnomes are four inches tall and have droll faces. The Danish consul gives his gnomes as gifts. "I'm doing something I enjoy—not for glory," Bill emphasizes.

The people Bill sees in the grocery store or the gas station or at church are inspirations for his carvings. "I find myself sitting in church, looking at features of people's faces. When they smile, there are certain wrinkles—there is a certain character. If someone asks me to make someone, I assure them the face won't look like the realistic face of a person. I'll take the head of one figure and put on the body of another."

A few years ago, Doris started helping with the painting. "Particularly on whimsical figures I trust her colors much more than mine," says Bill. "If on a figure of a particular occupation, then we have to agree. This is the way it should be. We talk it over."

Although he is German and Cornish by heritage, Bill likes carving in the Scandinavian style, and he enjoys visiting Sweden. "If there are woodcarvers in the area, we make a special effort to check them out and to learn from their experiences. I have high regard for old-world quality. I pride myself on obtaining the knowledge of old-world quality, when things were done by hand no matter what the country. All of this has made me more cognizant of carvers in Scandinavia. I wouldn't go there without looking up something in carving. That would be a must."

Everything about Bill's workshop is neat, organized. It's the same with his carving. There's the thought that one of his own occupations, cutting lady's dresses in the garment business,

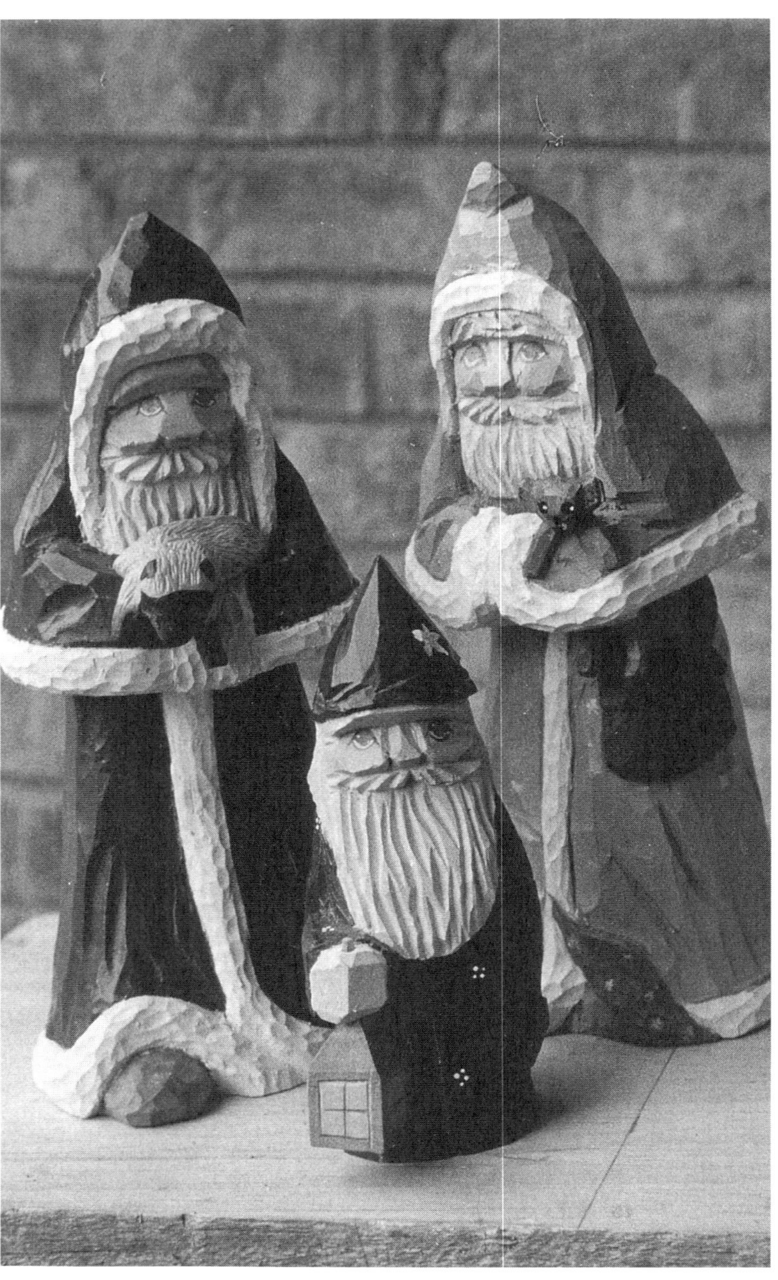

Santas are a favorite for Bill to carve.

contributed to this. "I never related it, but it was a precise operation," he notes. "I learned precision."

Although Bill carves mainly for enjoyment, he sells at the Holzfest, which is held in the Amanas in August, and at the Swedish-American Institute's Midsummer Festival in Minneapolis. Seeing people's reactions to his creatures is a moment he covets.

"The thing I look forward to most is the pleasure of pleasing people ... seeing their faces light up. ..."

Bill says that he has slowed down a bit. "I don't carve as heavy as I did four or five years ago. But hardly a day goes by that I don't carve something. Today I carved a couple of hours. It's a rarity that I don't carve three or four hours a day—except Sunday."

As he thinks about the future, he considers the unknowns. He has had carpal tunnel syndrome in both hands. "What scares me is that my eyes are going. I'm getting to the age of cataracts."

There is little doubt as Bill sits enjoying a glass of iced tea with Doris in their backyard that he is happy with his life. The "second" part of his life is richer than the first, he notes. Only recently did the Warricks give up their post-war bungalow on Des Moines' north side, where they lived forty-four years while raising their two children. "I don't feel guilty. I don't feel we live extravagantly, even though we live well, as long as we give time, talents, and treasures in service."

His recollections switch back to the Indiana childhood home, where there was no car, no running water, no inside bathroom. Four children slept in one bedroom. "I think back to my parents. Retirement was a dream. Here we are in retirement. That's when I give thanks for all the things I've got. Thanks for the grace of God. It could have gone another way. It strengthens your faith."

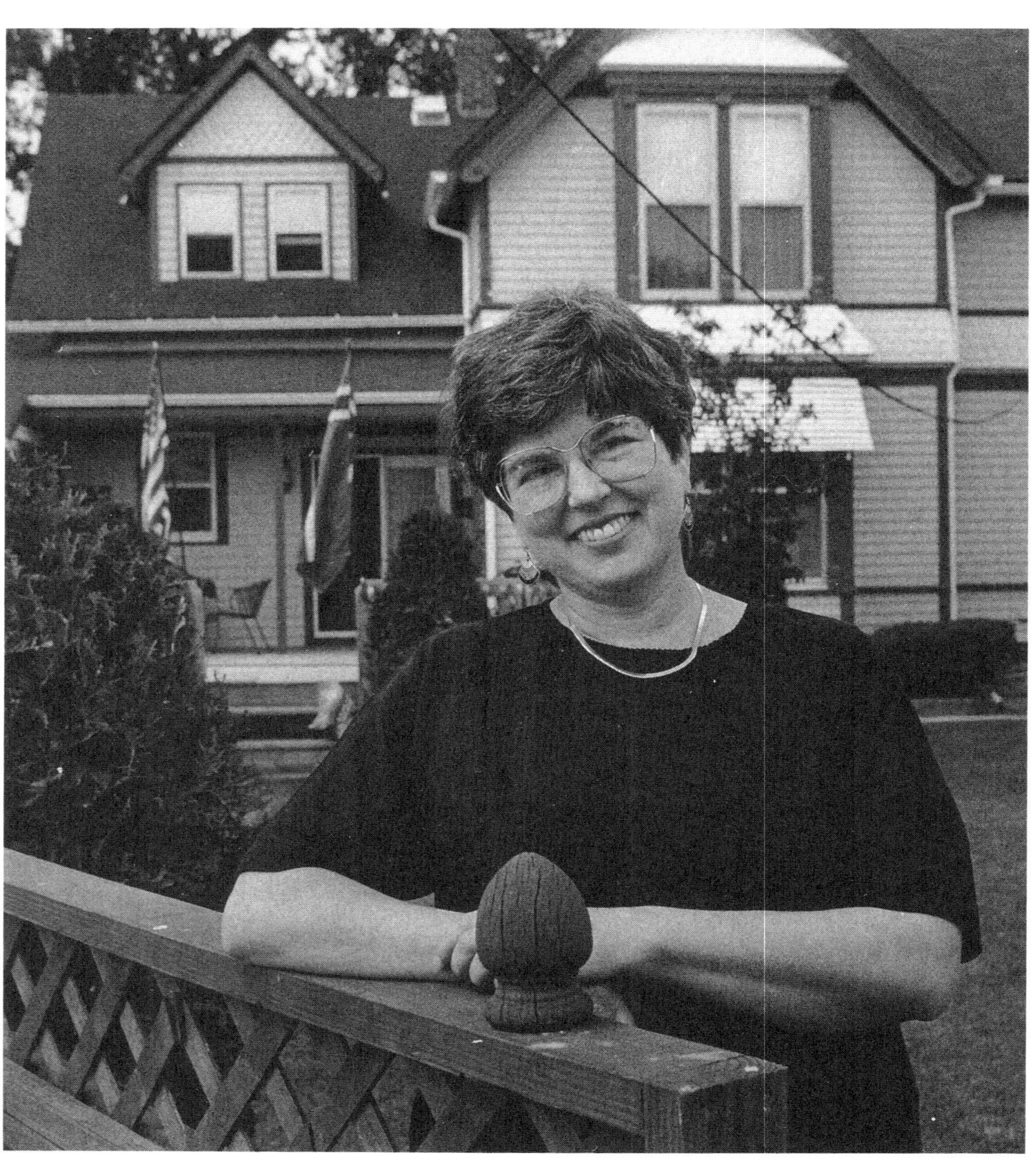

RUTH GREEN

Ruth Green: "I have chosen to develop designs that are symmetrical and use color-shading to shape the design. Line work and overlay strokes add detail to the designs.

"I work out the design on tracing paper then transfer the design to the prepared wooden piece. Rosemaling designs 'grow' from a root, which may be a scroll or flower form. I use three values (shades) of each color—dark, middle, and light. The colors are applied using C- or S-shaped strokes to fill in the design. With oil paints, the three values are applied side by side then blended together using the proper strokes. If using acrylic paints, the middle value is applied; the dark and light values are then 'floated' over the middle shade of the color. Overlay strokes decorate the flowers, leaves, and scrolls; line work ties the design elements together. As with anything you wish to do well, it takes much practice! But the practice pays off with decorated pieces you enjoy creating and sharing with others."

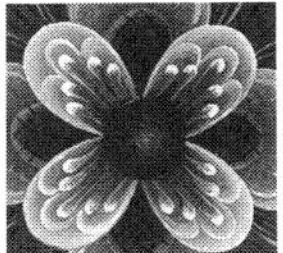

Ruth Green sits at the upstairs window of her yellow Victorian house, a short walk from downtown Decorah, the historic Norwegian town in northeast Iowa. Through the organdy curtains she looks out at tall trees, their green leaves fluttering in the breeze. It is Sunday afternoon, and Ruth is meticulously painting intricate flowers on a wooden box. This is the art of rosemaling, the distinctive rural Norwegian decorative folk painting.

Lined up neatly on her desk are tiny brushes, and on a palette, hand-mixed dabs of oil paint. Apparent are colors that make her pieces so distinct—blues and blue greens. This art, two centuries old, is one that Ruth has devoted the last twenty years to perpetuating. Anyone in this hilly town, where some still speak the language of the old country, will name Ruth as one of the great rosemaling artists in the area today.

To have such respect as a rosemaling artist in Decorah is like being a master in an art in a European village. This is a town where people know good rosemaling just as they know good *krumkake*. On their coffee tables, many have old pieces of rosemaling that were brought to the New World by great-grandparents.

Ruth has been a steadfast and assiduous artist. In fact, for a few years she worked at the folk art full-time. "My youngest was three years old when I started. I could give him a box of pens and paper, and he'd sit at the table with me and draw. Then I painted late at night when the kids were in bed. When they were in school, I'd paint during the day."

It was during this time that she and her husband, Dennis, a warm, friendly, solidly built, blond Norwegian, tried to make their living with their hands. Dennis, who grew up in the house where they now live (it had been his grandmother's), had dabbled at woodworking for years. When Ruth started rosemaling, he started supplying her and her students with lovingly crafted basswood bowls, boxes, and plates she needed for her art.

Soon, Ruth was going to conventions around the country, teaching and selling rosemaling; Dennis was renting booths at the same conventions and selling his carefully crafted basswood-turned ware to other painters. "We were very poor,"

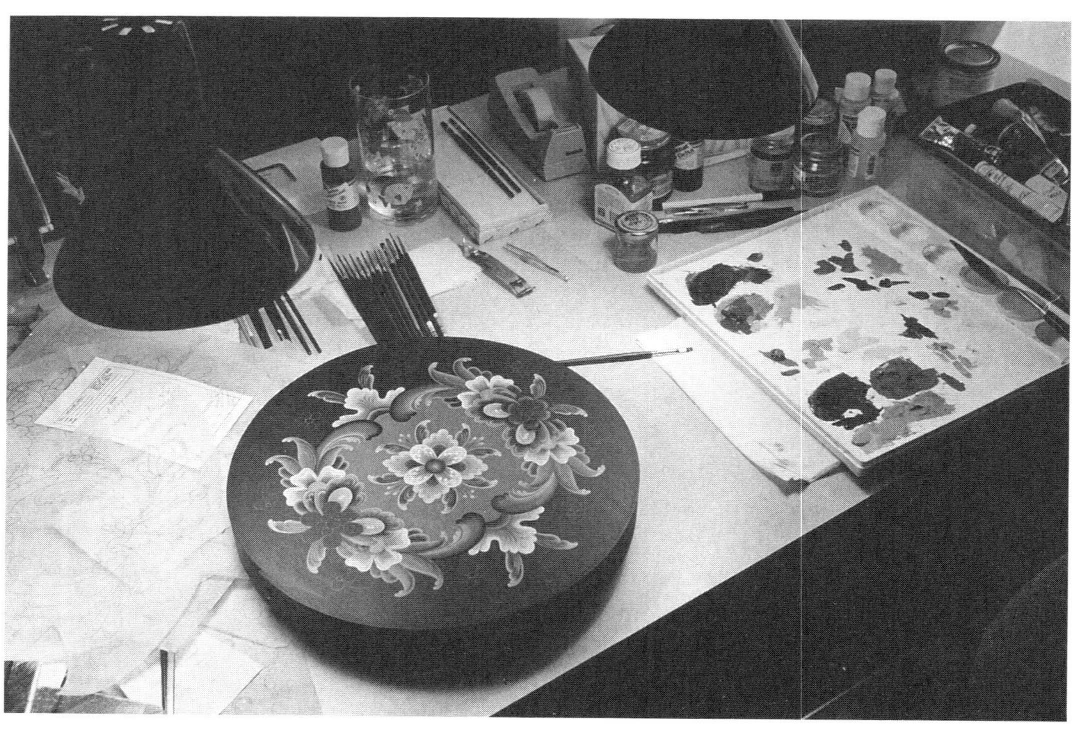

Dennis recalls. "You work for yourself, and you work harder than working with someone else. We needed security, and that came with having a regular job."

"Doing it full time was too much," Ruth remembers. She took a job as secretary in the nursing department at nearby alma mater Luther College, and she pulled back from the art for a while. Dennis went into real estate as an appraiser and seller.

Now she has balanced the art and the work into the serenity of self-satisfaction. The work at Luther gives her financial security and a break from her art. At night and on weekends she paints. "My life is made up of going to bed, getting up, working at Luther, coming home, rosemaling, going to bed, getting up, working at Luther, coming home, rosemaling ...," she recites in a quick, unconscious way. "That's probably why I went to work—to break it up so I wasn't doing my artwork exclusively. I could see I would eventually get burned out."

The Vesterheim Museum, the largest museum in the United States devoted to a single ethnic immigration group, is in Decorah. Rosemaling classes at the museum in the 1960s were a major impetus to reviving this art form in the United States.

IOWA FOLK ARTISTS

Twenty years ago, Ruth took a class at the museum taught by Vi Thode of Stoughton, Wisconsin, who in 1970 received gold medal status in the annual national competition sponsored by the museum. Now Ruth gives seminars at the museum.

It wasn't until she took the class from Vi Thode that Ruth realized she had absorbed so much of her Norwegian heritage. Ruth was born in Albert Lea, Minnesota, just north of Decorah, but as a child she didn't think much about her Norwegian roots. She had watched her grandmother paint simple floral designs on furniture. These "probably had their roots in rosemaling." A friend of her grandmother did rosemaling. "I didn't know anything about rosemaling when I was growing up. When I started taking rosemaling, I saw the connection with what I had growing up and didn't appreciate until I was an adult."

She recalls she had an interest in art as a child—particularly painting. She used to design clothes, which her mother would sew for her.

Her heritage, a love of painting, and natural patience blended to create an affection for the folk art. "I had not a clue when I started it, but I liked the way Vi painted. I liked her colors, the way she shaded, and the designs she used."

Ruth, whose merry light blue eyes contrast her dark hair, has the calm of one at peace with herself—something she needs for rosemaling. "It takes time and patience and a lot of practice," she says. "Rosemaling is made of stroke work. You have to know stroke work to do rosemaling."

She explains that rosemaling is made up of scrolls—fantasy-style flowers. The style she learned from Vi Thode and enjoys is based on flower forms from the Rogaland area of Norway. The flower forms, which stay the same from piece to piece, include the tulip, bonnet lily, and round flower.

Ruth creates her own designs, and to find the elements that go into these, she

Ruth's rosemaling is based on the flower forms of the Rogaland, Norway, area.

often visits museums in search of old pieces. She also studies old photos and books in pursuit of designs that she can bring back into existence—but with her own style. "I take my ideas from old rosemaling and adapt it to the colors I enjoy working in and adapt it to the way I enjoy painting. I don't like to copy the old and make something look old. ...

"I need to understand how the rosemaling design is put together that goes from style to style. I need to understand the elements of design—the scrolls and flower forms."

She admits that getting the right design can be a struggle and it takes time. "It takes a while to find a design I feel comfortable with before I put it on wood. Each drawing takes a long time to do. Sometimes, it comes together. Sometimes, I can see what is happening in a few days, and sometimes, it takes weeks and months."

She makes a tracing of the wooden piece on tracing paper and draws the design. When she finishes the pattern, she transfers it to the wooden piece. All the time she is studying, criticizing.

"I saw her take a design off three times before she centered it on a piece," mentions Dennis, who is a perfectionist himself with his woodworking. "I looked at it and couldn't tell it was not centered. She can look at a piece of someone else's and see if it works or doesn't work."

Her work is distinct because of the paint colors she mixes. She uses three values of each color—dark, middle, and light— and then blends them together. As she is painting, she will add an overlay stroke. Through an emphasis on shading peculiar to the Rogaland area, her rosemaling looks different from other styles. "I do less detail on top of the rosemaling because of the shading," she says.

All of this takes not only patience but time. It recently took her fifty hours to paint a chest. "I don't think about it. I'm always thinking about how I could do better."

Her video, *Rosemaling with Ruth Green—Rogaland Style,* is one in the series *Handwork School Educational Series,* put out by the Vesterheim Museum.

For Ruth, as an artist, the distracting struggle to find good wood is replaced by the inner peace of knowing that, if she needs a certain style box, all she has to do is ask Dennis. If, in two weeks, she needs bowls for the students in the class she is teaching, she only has to mention it to him.

Dennis stands in the large, organized woodworking studio behind the house. He picks up one of his perfectly turned bowls and explains that it was made from basswood, a tree that is native to northeast Iowa and a wood that painters like. He points out that he fills all the screw holes. Artists appreciate the care he puts into his work. He sells his pieces to painters in every state and Japan.

He buys rough-sawn and kiln-dried boards 103 inches long, rips them to the width he needs, reglues them, and sends them through the planer to get the correct thickness. Then he cuts the wood to the dimension he wants and mounts the

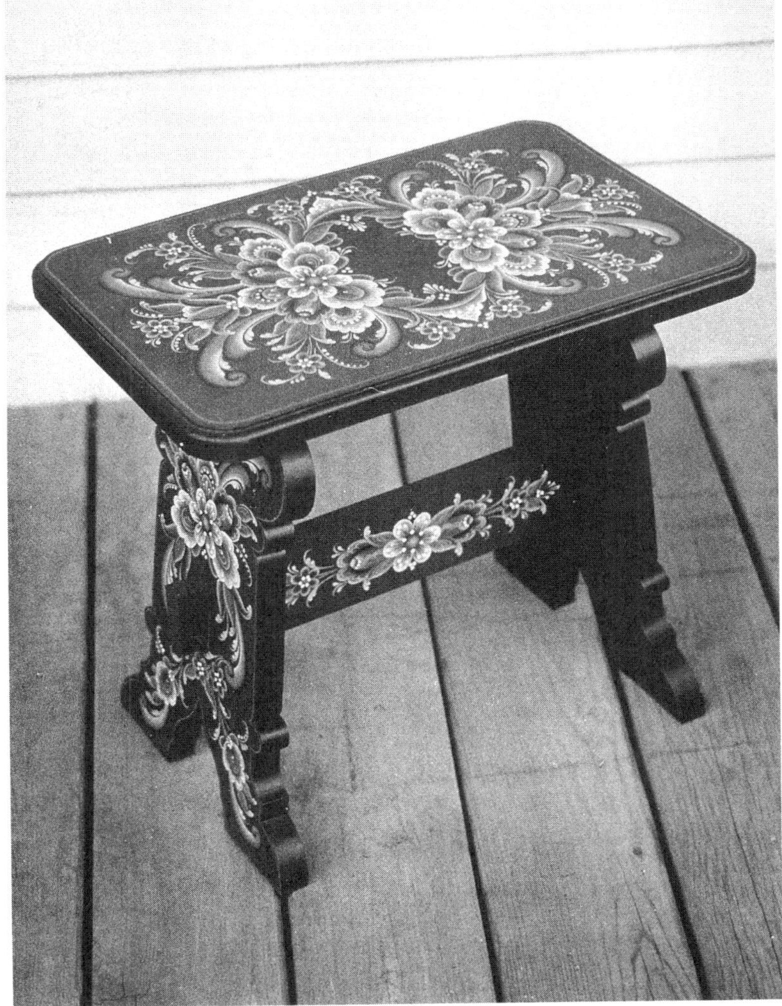

Ruth decorated a stool made by her husband.

piece on the turning lathe to shape it. "It takes longer to get the wood prepared than to turn," he says.

Ruth and Dennis are a team; their years together have made them unconscious, easy. Ruth is quiet, pensive. Dennis is energetic, gregarious. They met in eighth grade in Decorah and have been married thirty-five years. It is obvious their relationship is based on a deep friendship and caring for each other that many never know.

They work together, apart. She works upstairs; he is nearby in his studio behind the house. He stops by Luther every day and takes her to lunch. It's the automatic gesture of two people who want to be with each other. He is constantly trying to come up with new designs for her and has just brought her a new wooden tray with unique handles. It is perched against the wall rather obscurely. He is waiting to know if she likes it.

"Sometimes I create a piece, and it's not what she wants, and I feel a little hurt," he admits.

Ruth smiles at Dennis warmly. "I've learned to say, 'What's possible?' I wouldn't be able to do it without him."

"When I get up in the morning, my life is varied," Dennis says. "If Ruth's teaching in two weeks, I have to get going. I have to make a tray or a covered bowl for each person."

They both admit that they don't mind the paralyzing blizzards Iowa winters can bring. They stay home and work. "The bad side is that we both work more hours than we should," he observes.

After they were married, they were away from Decorah for a few years in Minneapolis, Fort Dodge, and big West Coast cities. They returned to Decorah so Dennis could finish coursework at Luther, and they did not expect to stay.

At first Ruth didn't like the familiarity of the small town where she spent time growing up. "I'm more of a private-type person. But there's a sense of support when there are hardships or catastrophes. Everyone cares about each other. That's what I like about a small town."

Surprisingly their house has few rosemaling pieces in it. "My joy of rosemaling is doing instead of living with it," says Ruth. "I'm not so attached that I want a lot around.

"We don't have to work all the time, but we do. I don't know why. We both enjoy what we're doing. We don't feel that much hardship."

Ruth's life has been constant, without interruptions of grief or sickness, and she's grateful for her good fortune. "My parents are still living. There have been no catastrophes that have changed the direction of life. We've been blessed."

She stops painting, looks through the organdy curtain to the hills beyond. "There's a peacefulness, whether it's raining or sunny, looking out the window. This is a place I can retreat. It's good therapy. I get absorbed in my painting, and other things go into the background."

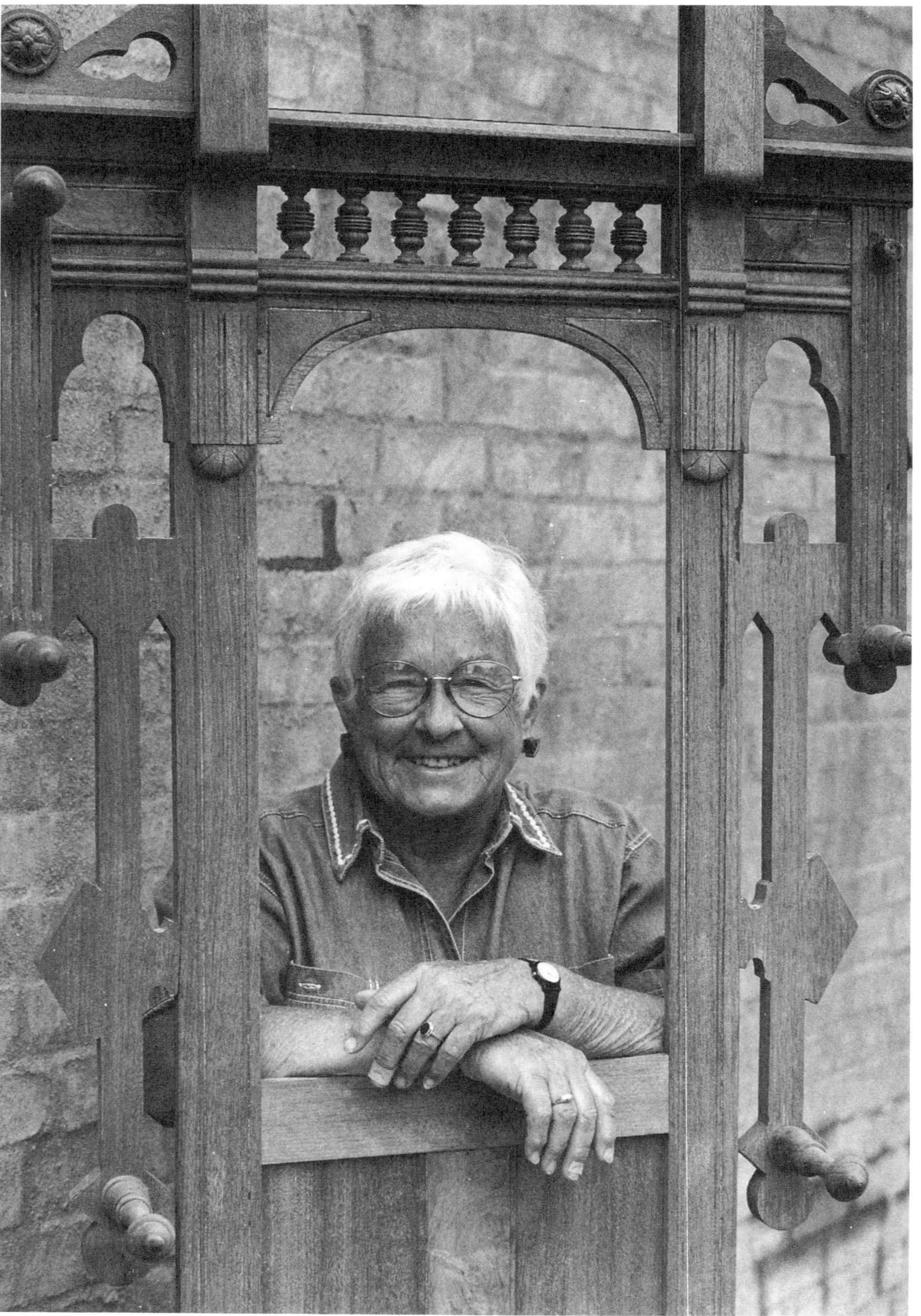

MARGE WEDGE MABLE

Marge Wedge Mable: "Start with a warm, sunny summer day, pack a lunch, and head for a boat moored at Saylorville Lake. Pull up to a cove, in the boat, where wind has deposited the wood. Gather choice driftwood. Scrub the dirt and mud from it in lake. Dry in sun. Head home, where base is sawed, arms attached with glue and nails, the body painted the base color with acrylic paint. Paint details (face, beard, mittens, belt, and fur) carefully. Attach a bell or star to one arm and/or a basket (made of reed on the boat). Cut stars from rusted tin. Each of other art pieces is gathered, sawed, glued, and created as the artist's eye dictates. Because each piece is one of a kind, there is no universal how-to method."

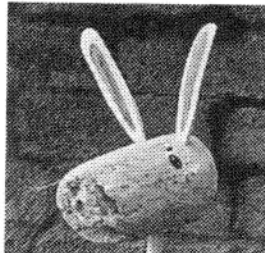

"Make do with what you have" is a maxim that has guided Marge Wedge Mable throughout her life. It has been the cornerstone of her whimsical driftwood folk art, and it helped her to raise five children as a single parent. "I was taught that you're not frivolous with possessions," she says. "You don't waste. That's the key."

It was during the rationing days of World War II, at her family's rustic summer camp, that Marge learned thriftiness. "We were taught frugality. I walked to the woods barefoot with a harness and brought the horses back. We didn't have a saddle. I learned how to milk cows. We raised vegetables, and the whole family canned. There was no electricity, and everything was done on a wood-burning stove and with a pump at the kitchen sink. We made do with what we had."

In 1968, four years after moving to Iowa from her roots in the East, Marge reinstated the make-everything-count rule. There was a divorce, and she was thrust into the role of a single mother raising five children between the ages of three and thirteen. She had never worked, "and I couldn't afford to move."

"We barely scraped by. We learned to shop at Goodwill. We got energy assistance for heat and qualified for government surplus cheese. If one night we had chicken, the next night we had garbage soup. That was creative use of materials. I cooked the bones and used vegetables. I kept the heat low. I put a light bulb in front of the thermostat so the room would think it was warm."

At the same time, she found relief from everyday problems by creating captivating objects out of odds and ends. "It was a release to keep busy, a way to fill in time that I might have spent with my partner. It was a way I could spend time with my kids—doing creative things."

Today, Marge, whose short white hair is striking against her summer tan, stands at the desk of Folkart, her shop on an old West Des Moines street. She is surrounded by her driftwood creations—an amusing large turtle, a dragon, Uncle Sams, snakes, birds, and rabbits. Behind her are shelves of fanciful driftwood Santas—each one different.

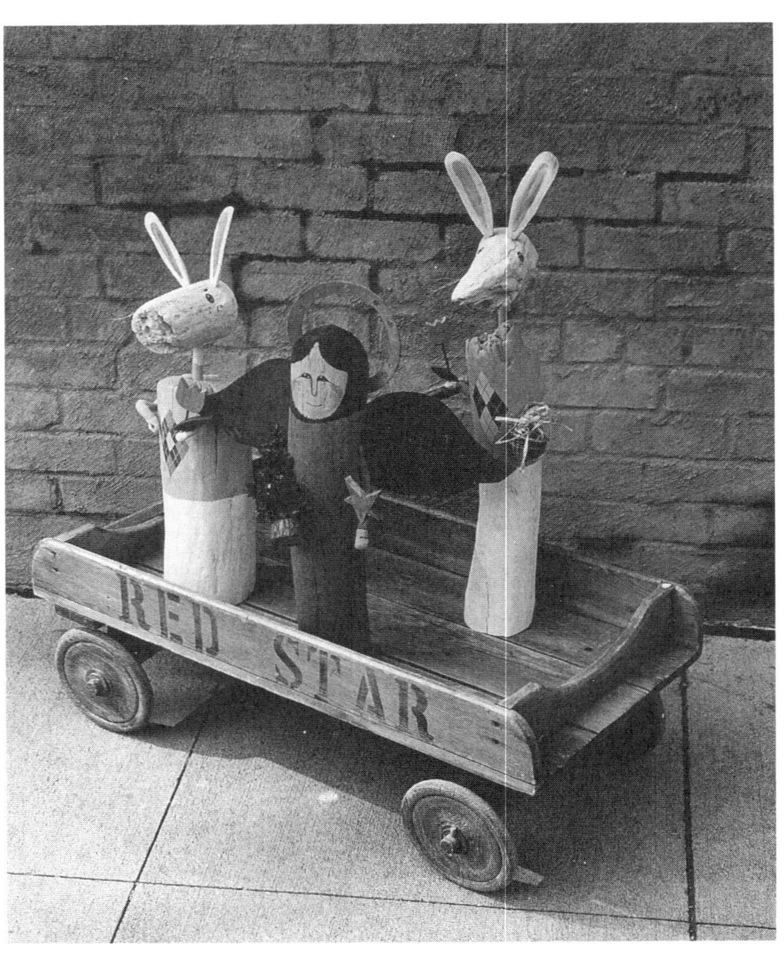

Driftwood folks stand in a wagon at the Folkart shop.

This curiosity about folk art had its origin in her early years. Her father had been a folk art painter. "He would sit down and encourage me to paint," she remembers. This pursuit was put aside while she attended Green Mountain College and majored in art. After she married, she looked for driftwood pieces when she and her husband went boating. "I'd make sea gulls. It was a natural extension of watercolors and oils I was using at the time."

She was so drawn to creating appealing subjects out of found objects that she started easing into folk art as a livelihood. While working half-time at the Johnston Public Schools, Marge found an intriguing old feed store for rent in the town. It had what she remembers as "primitive features." With her restless, creative energy she rented it the summer of 1969, renamed it the Iron Gate, and put in things she had made "that

IOWA FOLK ARTISTS

leaned in the folk art direction." These included primitive
paintings and carved pieces.

"Between customers I always had a project going as far as
painting or carving or whatever. There was an upstairs, and
Jackie and Jill [her oldest daughters] started a store called the
Bird's Nest. Everything they did was in citrus colors. They were
making little booklets, bookmarks, little paper things. Out of
pity people bought things from them." Marge supplemented
child support by teaching adult education courses, as well as
private classes at the shop.

More a creative venture than an income maker, the shop
was closed two years later. Marge eventually went to work
part-time in the dress department at Sears. She stayed until
1983. "It was fun being with people," she says. "I didn't totally
dislike it, but it wasn't my thing."

In 1981 Marge and youngest son, David, drove East to
spend time at the family camp. "He learned you don't turn on
the TV, and he started carving. I was carving wooden dolls
with joints, a new thing for me."

When she returned to Des Moines, Jackie—who had married Russ Leckband, potter at Living History Farms (Chapter
11)—was making dolls out of fabric. The vision of a shop was
revitalized, with Russ's pottery, Jackie's rag dolls, and Marge's
jointed dolls. "In November we rented a space for November
and December and hung the sign, 'Folkart.' The landlord
wanted us to take it for six months, so we compromised with
three."

The day after Christmas, an editor from Meredith Publishing Company walked into the store and bought the design for
one of Marge's tree ornaments. "That paid for the January
rent," Marge remembers. "We kept going month to month by
faith—Russ's pottery being the piece that held the shop together." She and Jackie took turns running the shop and basically still do.

It was four years later when son Skip, who was working in
Pennsylvania, called his mother and asked her to enter a ju-
ried show there. Since Marge was in Des Moines, he invited
the juror to his house to view Uncle Sams and flat wood Santas she had sent to him through the years. He set them out on
his kitchen table. The juror, impressed, invited Marge to be in
the show.

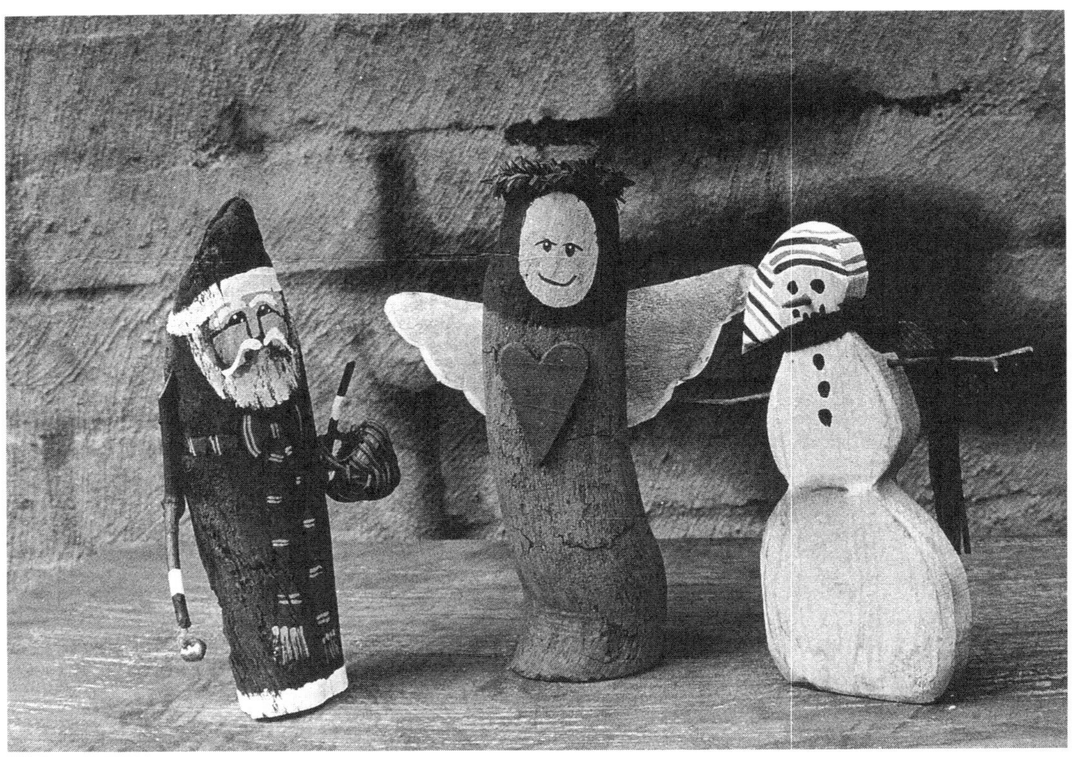

Marge immediately started worrying about what to put into the show. "There was a piece of driftwood beside me on the workbench as I was cutting out a Santa from flat wood. I looked at it and thought that it would be good as a Santa if I made the bottom flat and had it stand up. I made twelve, put them in the show, and charged what I thought was way out of line. They were gone by noon."

She returned to Des Moines excited about making figures from driftwood. "I came back, climbed all over Saylorville gathering driftwood. I made a lot of Santas that year, was amazed people bought them, but they were unique. They weren't in their collections yet."

She sold enough of the Santas, their postures and arms dictated by the shapes of the driftwood, that she could afford a pontoon boat. "I go out, pull up to the beach, and gather driftwood."

"When I first started the shop, I would take a pad to bed with me at night. I'd lie in bed and sketch ideas. One night it was rabbits, and I sketched ideas related to how to make rabbits. I'm up at 5 a.m. if there's an idea that needs to get done.

Or it could be 3 a.m., or I have stayed up. Ideas dictate the hours."

There is a primitive uniqueness to each piece. There is no copying. "I use driftwood for my canvas. I try to be original. I feel that people are depriving themselves of the thrill of being creative when they copy."

Marge's life has been a search for discarded objects that in her mind can be transformed into something enchanting. "I can't look at a rusty piece of metal in the road without picking it up. I can't go boating without picking up driftwood." She and a grandson found two huge logs in Saylorville Reservoir. "One's going to be a Santa with a pack on his back and an angel with wings. My grandson will do an abstract, colorful wall hanging. I didn't get a whole lot," she muses. "It was windy, and I had a boatload of grandkids."

She uses the same face on all of her pieces. "It was a face that struck me as being a kindly, caring image and what I wanted to project. It seems to fit Uncle Sams and Santas and fishermen. The eyes are the key that people seem to think others aren't able to capture."

The main carving she does on her Santas is on the arms. On other creations she carves other parts—some parts calling for more carving than others. She does the basic construction and some carving of her Santas and other creatures at home. She paints and also attaches the pieces at the shop. Sometimes her boat is her studio. "Everything is out there—including nature," she notes.

Marge believes folk art helps one look at life in a happy way. "Folk art helps keep a sense of humor and a sense of balance. The more I did, the more fanciful I got. I would stretch my imagination more—the more I saw the wood."

Marge taught her children early to make things out of odds and ends of ma-

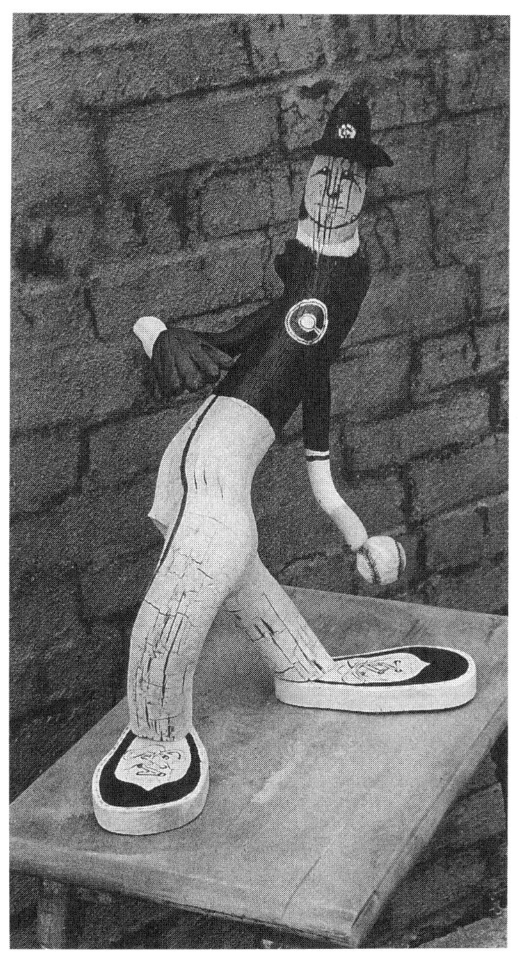

To Marge, this piece of driftwood suggested a baseball player.

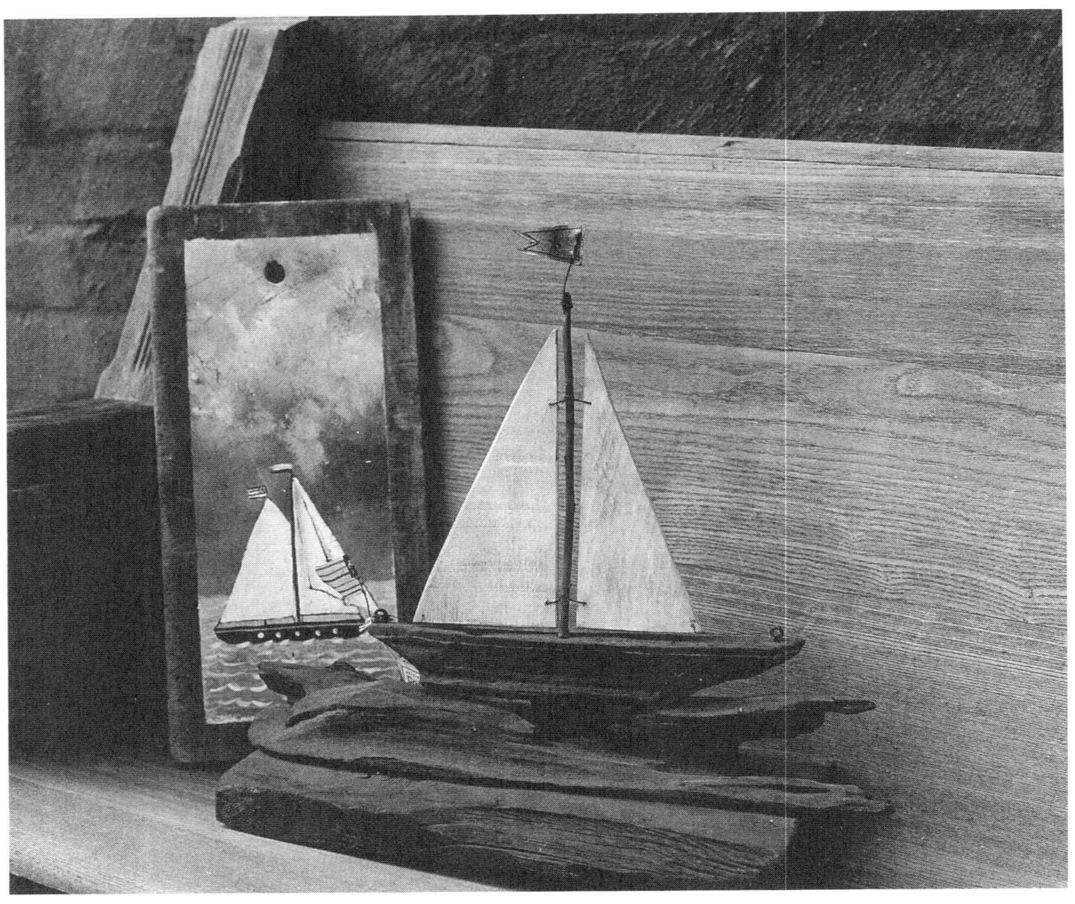

terials, and they are still doing this. "I taught them that, to be creative, they needed to use materials in different ways." Today they are all working in arts. Jackie decorates pottery for her husband Russ, Jill Clark makes wooden fish and fish decoys, and Betsy Peterson makes fanciful Humpty-Dumptys and other creatures. David is a photographer, and Skip, a graphic artist. The shop features works by Betsy, Jackie, Jill, and David. Skip designed the brochure.

"Each child is in some way in the shop. It's a really neat feeling. I did something right. Besides that, I like my kids." The shop is also a family center.

Betsy, whose whimsical figures have her mother's influence (the gangly arms) but whose style is decidedly her own, tells anyone who mentions her creativity, "My mom taught me. I started when I was a little, tiny girl. She would teach art classes, and I'd wander in and out. She'd have me step in

IOWA FOLK ARTISTS

paint and squeeze clay. She'd make our plates at suppertime have different colors and textures. She cared what color the wall was and what music she played. In the midst of what she was going through, she did that for us."

For a long time Marge felt a longing for her roots in the East. Sometimes, she thought she would move back there. That has changed. "I've always fought being happy being in Iowa. I left my family and friends living back East. But I'm absolutely content. Life is good. My heart beats with contentment.

"My whole life fits together now. I do all the things I love doing, and I make income. I love paint. I love water. I love creating, and I love people."

She stops and looks toward the ceiling. "I couldn't have done it without God. He's been walking beside me."

From nowhere she mentions Grandma Moses. "I've come full circle. I have a yen to paint on a flat surface (like I did as a child). I tend to be painting water scenes. That's reverting to childhood. That's my vicarious way of going home."

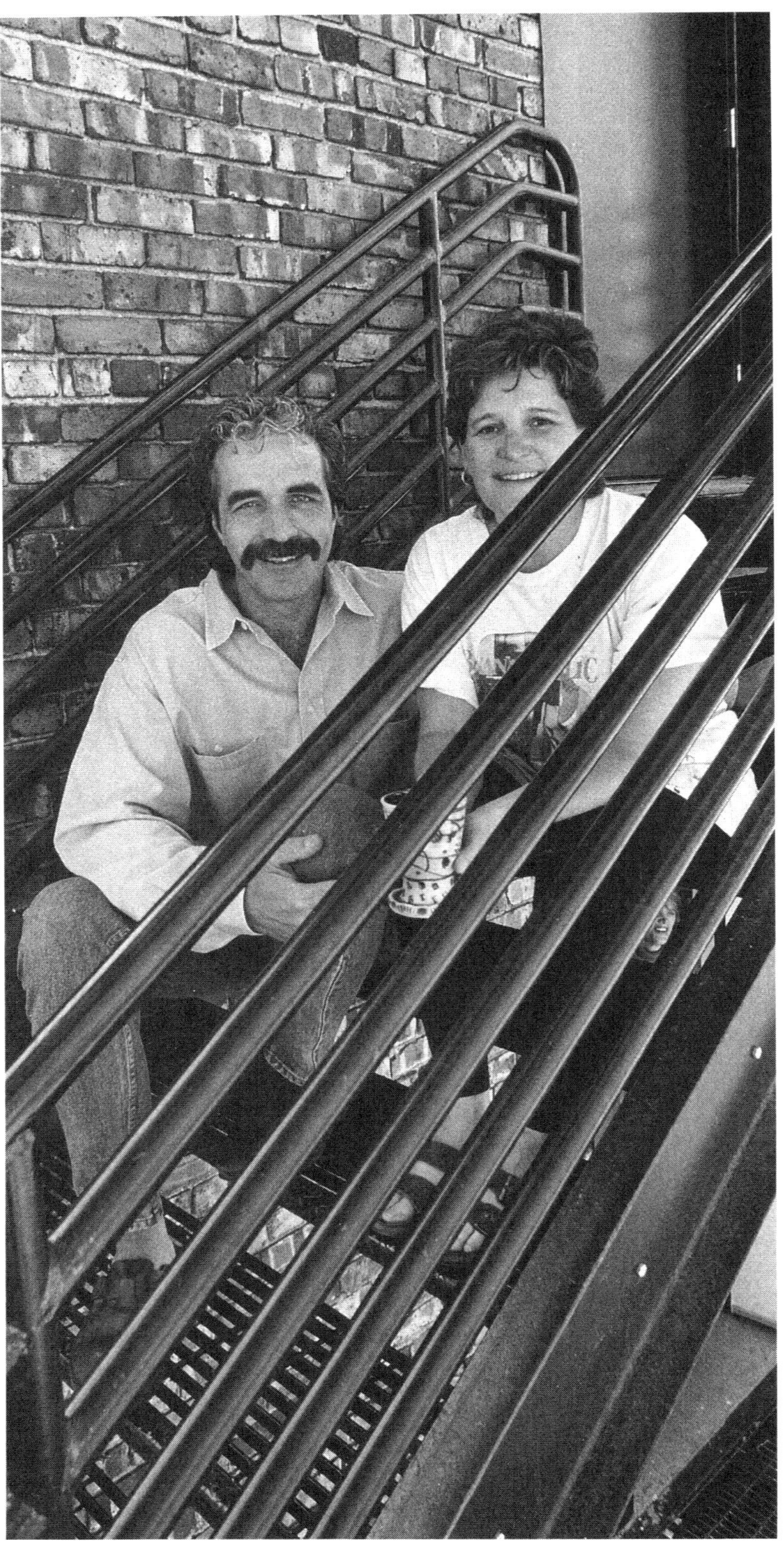

Sticks (Sarah Grant-Hutchison and Jim Lueders): "It starts in the shop. Each piece is handcrafted using birch ply and poplar woods, incorporating the logs and sticks that are found along our local waterways and in wooded areas.

"From this point Sarah draws the surface design on each piece in pencil, which in turn is woodburned to delineate the surface design. The pieces are then stained with either a black latex stain or a wood stain to seal the pieces and to help the paint adhere.

"We use acrylic paint. The pieces are individually hand-painted by one of twelve artisans. The paint is mixed with other colors to create the unique colorations in a loose technique that makes Sticks what it is.

"After the piece is painted, it goes to the finishing department, where a water-based polyurethane is applied—one to two coats. Tables and larger furniture pieces have three or four coats. This seals the pieces as well as protects. Also, in the

SARAH GRANT-HUTCHISON AND JIM LUEDERS

Sarah Grant-Hutchison stands in the middle of the fourteen-thousand-square-foot Sticks studio in an old brick warehouse in Des Moines. She is hand-buffing a chess set, piece by piece, that she has been painting for two days between countless interruptions. She admits that she is tired, and when she is tired, she sands and paints. "I felt like painting instead of drawing. I love drawing. If I'm down, I don't draw much. I do something else."

Her hands rest for a minute. Behind her is a stack of unpainted mirrors on which she will eventually draw. She looks at the figure in her hand. "I'm going to paint this weekend. We're so far behind."

Sarah has a one-hundred-mile-an-hour mind that can oversee several projects at once. She seems to know if there's an unfilled order or a whimsical wooden angel that doesn't yet have wings. Her energy ricochets around the room. Through working endless hours she manages to draw on every piece that leaves the studio for customers all over the country.

Jim Lueders, tall, rough-cut, and handsome in a Clint Eastwood sort of way, walks up silently beside her, a cup of coffee in his hand. He has an everything-is-all-right calmness. There is a phone call. He walks away momentarily, self-assured, unhurried. He is the other half of the creative team behind the Iowa-created phenomenon known as Sticks.

It is these two people bringing dissimilar experiences and distinct skills to a craft that makes it rare. Sarah is the sophisticated, trained artist. Jim is the untrained artist, the folk artist. Thus, their creations are enhanced by this unusual mesh of folk art and fine art against the backdrop of the Iowa culture.

Sarah grew up in Ames, fascinated by "architectural stuff"—blocks and Legos. "I drew constantly—line drawings of cities and houses and the inside of houses. I couldn't draw people or princesses or hands. I loved the structural environment and putting people in it. I wanted to be an architect."

She grew up in the university town, where her grandfather had been a university doctor. Her father, John, was a surgeon,

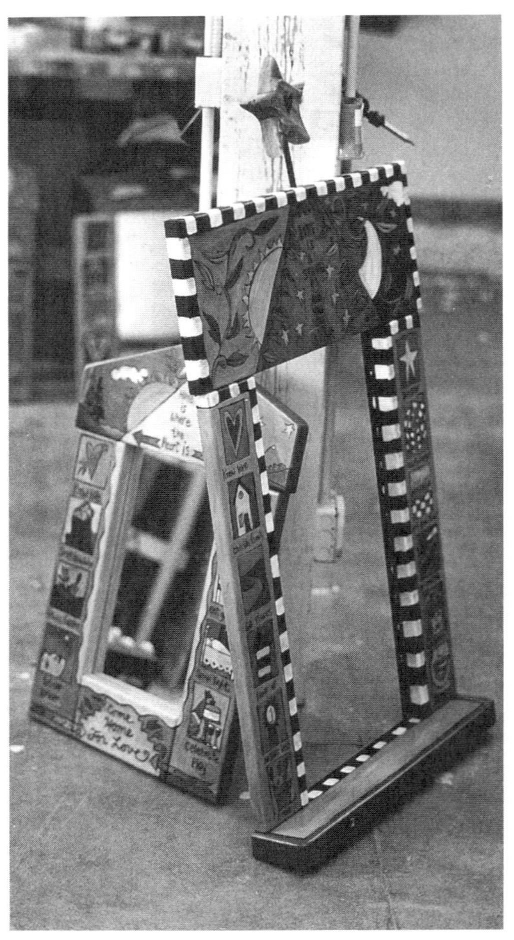

Mirrors stand finished in the Hutchison-Lueders studio.

her mother, Carol, a civic leader. At competitive Ames High Sarah wanted to "jump higher, run faster, organize everything, and know the answers." "That's how I am," she says matter-of-factly. She excelled at Colorado State University, getting three degrees: a bachelor and master of fine arts in print making and a master of fine arts in painting.

After college Sarah, who was teaching at Iowa State University, was asked by a friend working for a magazine to design a Nativity scene. She created one by burning and painting wood. "Everybody loved it," she remembers. "The Nativities turned into fish, animals, Santas, and for five years, by myself, I sold at a couple of art fairs here and there." Working under the name Origins, she drew directly on the pieces with a woodburner. "I didn't have the wherewithal to do sculpture." She would soon find her sculptor.

As a child growing up in Omaha, Nebraska, Jim Lueders was captivated by art. He constantly drew, painted, whittled, and struggled to learn more. "When I was in sixth grade, I talked my parents into letting me take an arts correspondence course. I paid for it with my paper route and mowing yards. My parents thought this was stupid. They were on me, and it was no fun."

In high school his art teacher encouraged this talent and helped him get through high school by setting up an art studio in the storage room at the school. "I'd go in and paint and draw," he recalls. On the side he was carving cars, little heads, and other shapes.

The summer he was fifteen, he helped his grandfather in Hardy, Iowa, fix up old farm buildings, including a farmhouse. "I saw from him there wasn't anything you couldn't do. I was proudest of the milk parlor we built out of concrete blocks. Mostly we fixed old barn doors. We moved a barbershop in Hardy. We picked the little shop up off its foundation so it faced the corner better. It was ten by fifteen. We had to

IOWA FOLK ARTISTS

break the whole thing off the foundation and jack it up and move it to another foundation."

For a time in the 1970s, he "ran around with no direction" before starting a business restoring tile and slate roofs on churches throughout Iowa. "It was an art that was dying out," Jim recalls. "People taking care of slate and tile roofs in this area had died. I learned how to do it. It's an old craft of knowing how to work with materials."

Jim met Sarah when she was teaching a drawing course at Des Moines Area Community College in 1986. "She was speaking about her paintings. She was making a living as an artist, and I wanted to get to know her. She had a studio. If I wanted to be an artist, I needed a studio."

Sarah and Jim take a break from too-much-going-on, sit next to each other in the middle of the studio, and reflect on their beginnings at Origins. "I hired him to be a painter," Sarah recalls. "What we found out was—with his construction background and his eyes—he was changing the pieces, making them more interesting in three dimensions. We started using logs. He was taking from sketches I'd draw. I had no idea how to make these into sculpture. When he moved into the studio, he brought lots of junk. We made something with lots of his junk. When we ran out of junk, we had to find more junk."

"We were plum out of flat stuff," he says.

"It was me pushing," adds Sarah. "I couldn't do cookie cutouts. I was going to quit or do something else."

Jim remembers going to a farm and "seeing interesting shapes in sticks." "She started drawing log Santas, and I started putting them together. My whole thing is making a palette for her to paint on."

"Many of the pieces I'm making have been in my head since I was a kid," Sarah declares. "I set off to find out how to do that. I found Jim who could do it for me."

And so, in 1991, Sarah and Jim converged imaginations to construct the amusing, entertaining, and educational mirrors, chess sets, chairs, boxes, angels, coatracks, Santas, trunks, and Nativity scenes that go under the catch-all company name Sticks. With a consortium half folk art (Jim) and half fine art (Sarah), the unusual, uplifting pieces project just that—the innocence of folk art and the sophistication of fine art.

"It's a mixture of the fact I'm highly trained and Jim sees things and makes them appeal to people," says Sarah. "I paint with my hands and big brushes. Using logs and found materials allows me to translate the painting method onto these pieces."

The log angels are charming, but it's the sticks and rambling wire plugged into angels' heads that give them magnetism. The Santas have large log bodies and smaller log arms and legs. The suits, buttons, and faces are painted on the logs. The hallelujah ladies, with their sky-reaching arms, are made from Y branches. Sarah remembers her dad saying, "As soon as I retire, I'm going out and look for Y branches. I never look at a Y branch without thinking of hallelujah ladies lying on the ground."

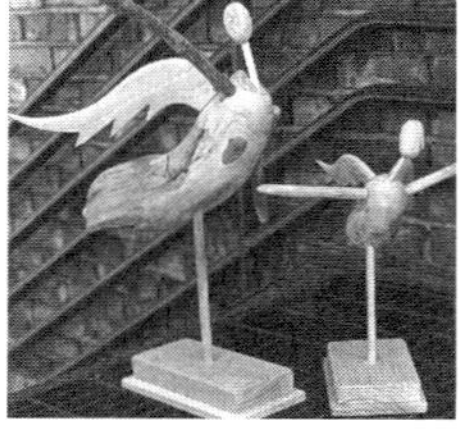

Sticks angels mix sophistication of fine art with the innocence of folk art.

Sayings on Sticks mirrors suggest how to live life.

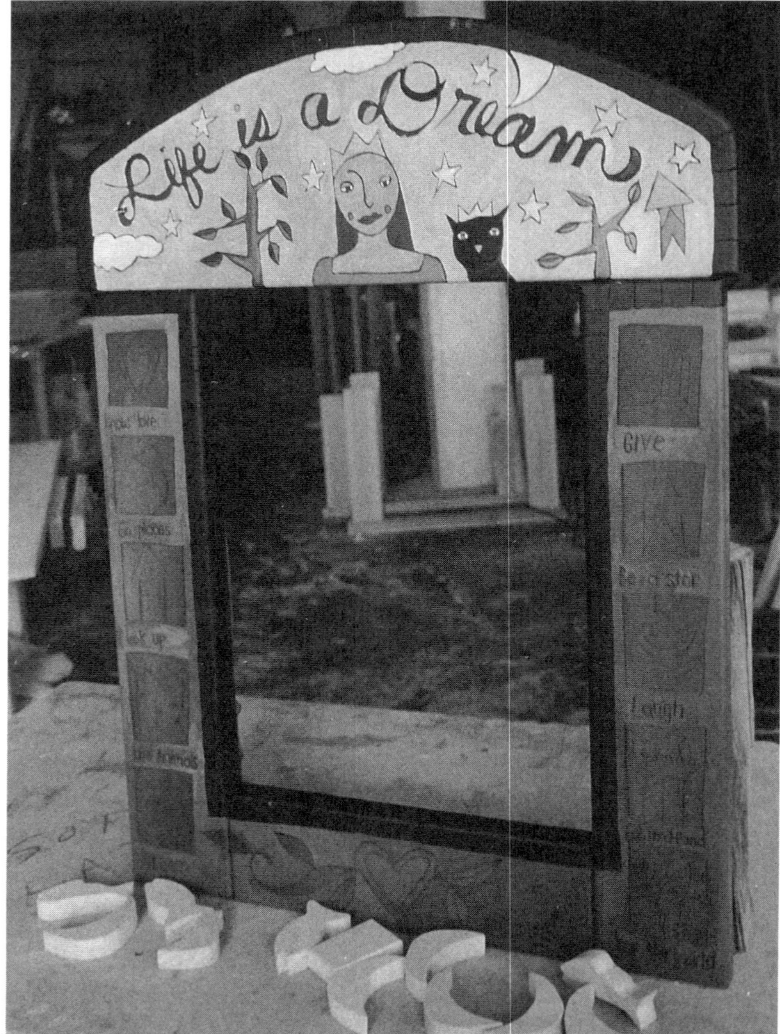

IOWA FOLK ARTISTS

It's Sarah's inspired everyone-has-heard-, life's-a-bowl-type expressions that make the objects endearing. They are uplifting, do-your-best-every-doggone-day guides to living life. "All the sayings come from my head," she says. "It spring-feeds in my head. I twist it around. It floats out in my pencil.

"It's what it feels like to live. It's a concept of wood and visual imaginings strung together to make you feel like a viewer of your life. I don't think of the viewer. I think of myself as the viewer. I think that everyone, no matter what has happened in a lifetime, experiences the same things. I talk about what's interesting to me, what I wish would happen. I twist into these things a lot of questions for people. I want the piece to initiate interaction for people in a room, not with the piece but with each other."

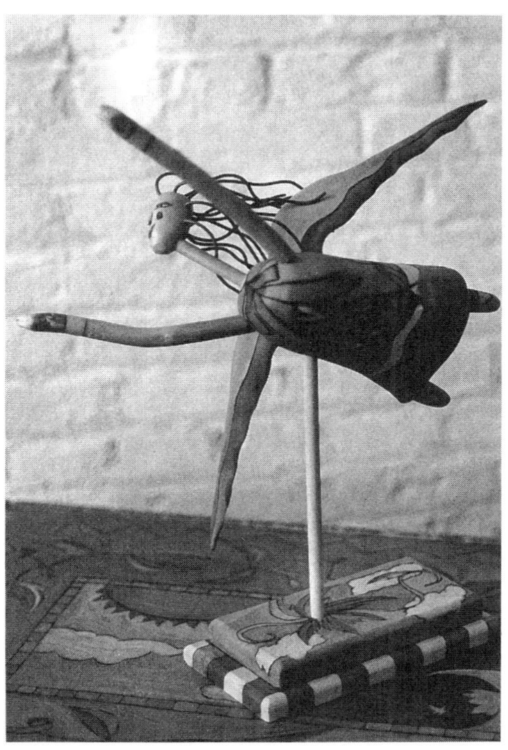

An angel sails through the Sticks studio.

For her this comfort with words and phrases started in her childhood home. "The whole thing of reading and language and the use of language within my family group has been quite sophisticated."

On vacation her family heard a weatherman say, "The weather is an iffy mixed bag of maybes." "My dad said, 'That's a mirror. Life's a mixed bag of maybes.' The farther and deeper I go in looking at the way words are put together, the more interested people are in what we do."

She credits her parents with giving her this aptitude for enjoying life and passing this joy to others. "Dad worked hard, was conscientious and fair. That's what I wanted to be. Mother is very bright. She has used smarts as a leader. Her leadership has influenced me. The responsibility I have to life and to everyone around me is what she has given me that goes into this work.

"The combination of these two people, with their work ethic and civic responsibility, has made the message in this work. I'm passing on the message."

To keep up with demand, Sticks employs some forty painters, woodworkers, shippers, and accountants. In reality these people are musicians, artists, journalists, and house-wives. "We are working collaboratively with each other and with a high-energy, talented group of people who otherwise would not find employment in art," says Sarah. "They have ideas, and we want them respected and recognized. What I do is fun, and the economic stability of the forty who work here has been established."

She tells about a cabinetmaker hired because of his mill-work experience. "He creates fancy mirrors. He has ideas on how things are put together. This comes from my love of teaching. It's like a graduate studio. I feel like a coach."

The bright loft-like studio has two floors. It is a place where everyone is working in an at-ease atmosphere. There is a congenial mix of ages.

The talents of Jim and Sarah are coming full circle to architecture. Using Jim's construction background and Sarah's childhood interest in architecture, the group is designing interior spaces—walls, furniture, chairs. They have done an emergency room at Blank Children's Hospital in Des Moines, a

This table illustrates Sticks technique.

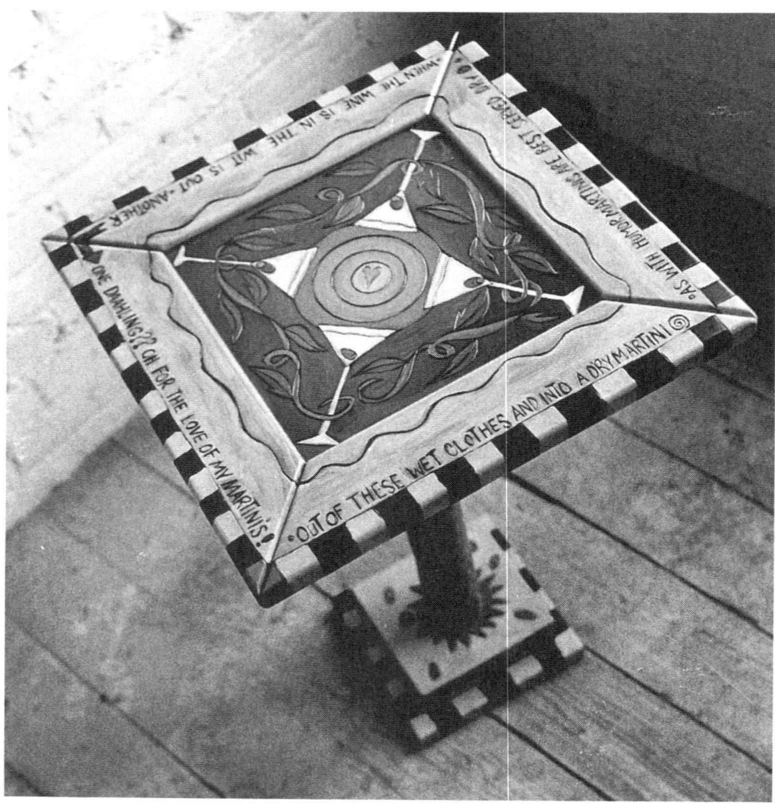

child care center at the Iowa State University School of Veterinary Medicine, a restaurant, and two suites in a hotel. Jim designs the structural pieces and oversees the installation. "From me doing this so many years I can communicate," he says.

For Sarah and Jim there is a tug between too much work and families. Sarah, a single mother, is raising Rachel, Rebecca, and Hannah and, at the same time, working sixty to eighty hours a week. Jim, also a single parent, is raising Abigail, Gabriel, Zebadiah, Jessica, Moirah, and Elijah, who are between the ages of seven and twenty-one. "The older ones help the younger ones," he comments. "They all have responsibilities they have to do every day. It rotates."

Today, Sarah and Jim can support themselves with the business, but there was struggle before that happened. "We have essentially built the business with a small loan from Dad and a small line of credit," says Sarah. "We didn't have cash flow. I didn't take home a paycheck. We had people on the payroll. We'd tell them to hold off. We had to wait for people to pay us."

It is obvious that they have fun creating, working. There is a never-ending give-and-take of ideas and thoughts between the two. Jim tells her it's a challenge to keep up with her. She sluffs it off, "He tells me that every day. He has bigger ideas than big. He's pretty laid back, pretty even."

Jim adds, "I'm the dreamer. I bring dreams down—Sarah's and mine—to reality."

Sarah picks up another chess piece, walks around the studio, and buffs. She is already thinking ahead. They're outgrowing the studio—they'd like to find an old barn near Des Moines.

BIBLIOGRAPHY

Fried, Fred and Mary. 1978. *America's Forgotten Folk Arts*. New York: Pantheon Books

Nelson, Marion, ed. 1995. *Norwegian Folk Art: The Migration of Tradition*. New York: Abbeville Press Publisher in association with the Museum of American Folk Art and the Norwegian Folk Museum, Oslo.

Ohen, Steven. 1988. *Remaining Faithful: Amana Folk Art in Transition*. Des Moines: Iowa Department of Cultural Affairs.

Refsal, Harley. 1992. *Woodcarving in the Scandinavian Style*. New York: Sterling Publishing Company.

———. 1995. *Carving Trolls and Other Scandinavian-Style Characters*. Decorah, Iowa: Dog Hill Press.

Schanz, Joanna. 1986. *Willow Basketry of the Amana Colonies*. Iowa City, Iowa: Penfield Press.

Todd, Leonard. 1976. "Cornhusk Dolls." *Americana*. Vol. 4, No. 5, November.

Zug, Joan Liffring. 1975. *The Amanas Yesterday*. Amana, Iowa: Amana Society.